Ten to One

Wesleyan Poetry

TEN

TO

ONE

Bob Perelman

Selected Poems

Wesleyan University Press

Published by University Press of New England

Hanover and London

Wesleyan University Press

Published by University Press of New England, Hanover, NH 03755

© 1999 by Bob Perelman

Printed in the United States of America

5 4 3 2 1

CIP data appear at the end of the book

This book is dedicated to Francie Shaw

Contents

Acknowledgements

Some of these poems have appeared in *Abacus, Aerial, Best American Poetry, Best of the Best American Poetry, Box Car, Colorado Review, Diacritics, Epoch, Fragmente, From the Other Side of the Century, Harvard Review, Hills, The Impercient Lecture Series, In the American Tree, Iowa Review, "Language" Poetries, Line, Lingo, Miam, Mirage, New American Writing, O-Blēk, Oink!, Onward, Paper Air, Poems for the Millenium, Postmodern American Poetry: A Norton Anthology, Postmodern Culture, Raddle Moon, Reality Studios, Shiny, 6ix, Socialist Review, Sulfur, Temblor, This, Tramen, 21 + 1:* Poetes amèricains d'aujourd'hui, *The Wallace Stevens Newsletter, Writing, ZYZZYVA.*

"Chaim Soutine" and *a.k.a* (parts 1 and 2) were published as chapbooks by Editions Hèrisson (Buffalo, N.Y.: 1994) and Tuumba Press (Berkeley, 1979), respectively.

"The Marginalization of Poetry" has appeared (among other places) in *The Marginalization of Poetry: Language Writing and Literary History* (Princeton University Press, 1996).

Introduction

Walter Benjamin imagined a perfect criticism that would only quote the material it studied. In trying to write this introduction I've increasingly felt the spirit of that desire—to get out of the way and let the poems speak, sing, make noise, counterpunch, loll & invite, do whatever it is they do. But writing, whether of poetry, criticism, theory, or whatever generic hybrid, is a pragmatic activity. So a few remarks might help these poems find new readers.

The first book represented here, *Braille* (1975), was culled from a year-long series of improvisations, inspired by reading Williams's *Kora in Hell* and, less directly, by Vallejo's *Trilce*. The next book, *7 Works* (1978), was written after I entered the Bay Area literary environment that would come to be known as Language Writing. Cut up and collage, which I noticed via Ted Berrigan, John Ashbery, and William Burroughs, were the ruling principles here. But, unlike in Burroughs's cut ups, the point wasn't to undo the *Time* magazine prose world. For me, writing "An Autobiography" with words from Mozart, Shackleton, and Stendhal was a way of sneaking up on a theatrically overdetermined representation of a person. Stitching together swaths of writing from different centuries made for more capacious emotional, psychological, and historical spaces than my own single could have generated.

While collage can display freedom from time and place, it can also display a skittish refusal of any location outside itself. How to speak to one's own time and place without simply reflecting it and locking into that apparent inertia? My later books take on this problem: in the contemporary environment of mass audiences and fragmented art audiences, sound bites passing for information, slogans passing for community, how to make new meaning that also points in a meaningful direction. Sound is crucial, as the site both of pleasure and of ideology; so are the perspectives that playing with form can provide. I want the sound of the poem and the form—the poem's 'plot'—to keep readers stimulated. (Form, in this sense, *is* more than an extension of content.)

Since I've mentioned Language Writing, I'd like to counter a common misunderstanding that sees it as denying meaning or reference. What I've gotten from my involvement with it is an appetite for poetic techniques—avant or not, as long as they're useful for trying to write the present. For instance, the following poem from *The Future of Memory:*

FAKE DREAM: THE LIBRARY

January 28: We were going to
have sex in the stacks. We

were in the 800s, standing eagerly
amid the old copies of the

Romantics. Looking at the dark blue
spines of Wordsworth's *Collected*, I thought

how the intensity of his need
to express his unplaced social being

in sentences had produced publicly verifiable
beauty so that his subsequent civic

aspirations seemed to have importance enough
for him to become Poet Laureate

and how his later leaden writing
upheld that intensity and verifiability, only

instead of searching wind and rocks
and retina for the sentences of

his social being, he chirped his
confirmed lofty perch to other social

beings in lengthy claustrophobic hallelujahs for
the present moment. There are devices

to keep it still, long enough,
and he had learned them. Rhyme

was a burden, crime was unambiguously,
explainably wrong, time had snuck around

behind him. He had carved his
own anxiety into a throne and

now he was stuck on it,
remembering sadder days when he had

wanted to be happy with a
purity that made him blink, thinking

back. He remembered in a trance:
the past seemed unbearably near. Our

more slippery, contrapuntal hallelujahs were planted
in the immediate future, only a

few buttons, zippers and a little
elastic down the road. We had

first snuck into the men's room
but it had been crowded with

two intensely separated men hunched at
urinals 1 and 6. We turned

to hurry out, and you pointed
to the magic marker graffiti on

the beige tiles: "This place needs
a women's touch" answered by "FINGER

MY ASSHOLE, CUNT!" This second message
had been modified by an arrow

indicating "CUNT" was to be moved
from behind to before "ASSHOLE": "FINGER

MY CUNT, ASSHOLE!" We were eager
to prove syntax was not mere

vanity and that bodies could use
it to resist the tyranny of

elemental words. And wouldn't it be
nice to get knowledge and pleasure

on the same page. So we'd
hurried out to the deserted 800s.

Like the title says, it's a fake dream. But the various writing situations
in it are true to the present. Wordsworth was almost a democratic poet,
almost an avant-gardist; for many of his contemporary readers I imag-
ine he embodied a self not beholden to inherited class horizons. But he
achieved this at the cost of an idealized Nature, mute and female, and
an infantilized sister (I'm referring to her image in his poems, not the
person Dorothy). And by the end of his career he was writing sonnet
sequences justifying capital punishment.

For living poets writing is closer to a graffiti situation than to inscrib-
ing the canonized pages of Wordsworth. Our pages are not pristine,
they're scrawled over with prior social postings, threats, blandishments.
From the vantage of the men's room, the particular snarl of shame,
rage, and threatened violence is all too familiar. Despite the poem's
humor and its messing around with narrative probabilities, I'm quite
serious about the need to resist the tyranny of elemental words. Which
are what? Jew? Serb? Woman? God? Cunt? Nature? Poetry? They're
words that brook no argument, that are intended to be outside of syn-
tax and thus outside of history. I try to resist these when I write. So I'm
all for that third graffitist—a woman? a man? gay? straight?—who drew
the arrows and critiqued the male threat, mocked it, began to undo it.
Elemental words are always a threat, to whoever's outside their slanted
beneficence. Resisting elemental words is a prerequisite to the pleasures
that poetry can offer.

I am against an elemental sense of poetry: as I write at the end of
Face Value, "This isn't eternity, have I said that yet?" This does not
mean that I imagine the present to be some kind of Hegelian or post-
modern or just plain dystopian "end of poetry." What's in this book is
nothing if not poetry. My allegiance is pledged. But poetry, for me, re-
mains alive by its insistence that there are no last words.

Philadelphia, July 5, 1999

Ten to One

PHILOSOPHICAL INVESTIGATIONS

Tongue through the door. I taste what I think and then it's available. A car's speed weeps, but this balances largely, large tottering stand always at you, this vocal existence. Life exists elsewhere as well. Pulse returning, hot on the trail.

Then there's the dainty look of a field being looked at. Ants busy, sky pitched. Or a three day rain, lap it up. On board the lap, leaving silence. Elsewhere elseperson announcing its else in bonged norms, the call of the universe.

CULTURE

Urge of rain greying the arches. Sad rome files out. The past gets small, hides under back yard pines, plays dead. Wonder where the ford broke its heart. Here some indians, there some settlers, in between, a river of perfume. So much for the trees.

Seeing them as others, the eye finds itself in birdland, lost, a masterpiece. And the desert squirrels on home to where you left it but can't go back for it. The ouch of pleasure, miffed by messy leaves. Here we shine for miles of forest.

Her rushes like ten arms invade the english ladies' gentlemen's hole agreement. Wandering amid vacationing boulders.

THE FORTUNE TELLER

You can enjoy the body. You can enjoy the vision of particulars as well, creeping inward through your peeping outward, like a snake into home room. You may obtain prompt, accurate motion from your muscles, and, with practice, can desire your bones to point the way they do. With practice! It grows on trees, you can't waste it! Your spending it *is* it! Practical!

There is information waiting when you open your mouth to lull the dog, or when you wake up inside the house again. And when you think, in the influence of gravity, sinking and rising at the same time, then there's a big kiss forming as you form your lips. So the time is now! The pattern of a lifetime! How meaning flies, roots, okays your next step! Shape! Congratulations.

RANT

You're it. The scene is set. More prizes. By this time
everyone had a claim out,
their vectors shaved the fuzz off

natura. You're it. The tightrope of feeling, neurotic
grooming, preparing to prepare, nature feeds
you. The explosion was extraordinarily you
and I said, if ever a tree was yellow,

if ever a private automaton invaded the sky, the prairie's Paris,
a sign to leap from the grave as pure behavior, then
you're tagged hard and boom goes the skin of thought,
wind is the ally, not air.

WE SEE

In the universities, in the supermarkets, in the language, everywhere society is spoken, we see people unable to dress themselves in human proportion, we see them fooled into cannibalism by sweet talk, we see them drawling on the beach, looking each other over, looking for fingerprints, yet at the same time they are clinically unable to identify their own assholes in a series of simple political mugshots, we see them irritated, searching . . .

AN AUTOBIOGRAPHY

Everyone keeps shouting in my ears. But rest assured, dear papa, that these are my very own sentiments and have not been borrowed from anyone.

Has the reader ever been madly in love? One does not load up on odds & ends on the chance of their proving useful. The utmost reduction compatible with efficiency is the first & last thing to aim at.

But I am putting off for too long a necessary statement. My mother was a charming woman and I was in love with her. One night, when by chance I had been put to sleep on the floor of her room on a mattress, this woman, agile as a deer, bounded over my mattress to reach her bed more quickly.

In loving her at the age of six (a charming place with handsome horses) I had exactly the same character as now, crusts & air spaces in layers. Bitterly cold wind & low drift. The surface terribly soft. My way of starting on the quest for happiness has not changed at all, with this sole exception: that in what constitutes the physical side of love (it froze hard within a very short time) I was what Caesar would be, with regard to cannon & small arms. I would soon have learned, and it would have changed nothing essential in my tactics. I wanted to cover my mother with kisses, and for her to have no clothes on. It was quite usual to feel one side of the face getting sunburned while the other was being frozen. A journey of this kind is no joke.

I abhorred my father. He brought with him memories of how it feels to be intensely, fiercely hungry. He came and interrupted our kisses. Be so good as to remember that I lost her, in childbed, when I was barely seven. You will easily conceive what I have had to bear—what courage and fortitude I have needed as things grew steadily worse between the depots. He came and interrupted our kisses. During the period from November fifteen to February twenty-three, he had but one full meal, and that on Christmas day. Even then he did not keep the sense of repletion for long: within an hour he was as hungry as ever.

I always wanted to give them to her on her bosom. Be so good as to remember that I lost her, in childbed, when I was barely seven. She was plump and looked forward to each meal with keen anticipation and an exquisite freshness, but the food seemed to disappear without making her any the less ravenous. The evening meal was pretty, only it froze hard in a very short time. My father became rather primitive when he was hungry—weakened, hopeless, spiritless; but my mother had an expression of perfect serenity, and, to conclude, she often used to read the *Divine Comedy* of Dante through in the original. Long afterwards, I found five or six different editions in her room which had remained shut up.

We could not joke about food. My aunt dared reproach me with not weeping enough! You can imagine my suffering, and what I felt! Besides, she took no part in love. She thought about it most of the time, and she used to talk about it, but always in the most serious manner possible. As for me, it was with strange feelings that I was 'as criminal as possible.'

I did not experience really severe hunger until I was much too preoccupied with the heavy and dangerous to be able to talk much. Those were silent days. I had been the first to be horrified by the sounds which I had produced. I would get up at 5 A.M. in order to make a start at 7 A.M., and would eat my scanty breakfast that only seemed to accentuate hunger. Then I would describe things in the good days to come.

The 'Wild Roll' was to be the high water mark of luxury. My hand refuses to write. I have been pacing around for a quarter of an hour. If I reduced myself to reasonable limits, I would be unjust to the frenzy of happiness, the excess of happiness . . . The only civilized experience that is akin to it is when one steps unknowingly on the pavement.

Her room remained closed for ten years after her death. No servants entered it. I alone had the key. My father was severely reprimanded. The moisture on his clothes froze hard. He sold them to build his new street and other follies. This ruined him.

"Now we are on board ship," he would say. "We wake up in a bunk, and the first thing we do is to stretch out our hands and get some chocolate, some Garibaldi biscuits, and some apples. We eat those in the bunk, and then we get up for breakfast. Breakfast will be at eight o'clock, and we will have porridge, fish, bacon and eggs . . ." His eyes were sparkling with rage. ". . . cold ham, plum pudding, sweets, fresh roll and butter, marmalade and coffee. At eleven o'clock we will have hot cocoa, open jam tarts, fried cods' roe, and slices of heavy plum cake. That will be all until one o'clock. Nothing can prevent madness."

Here I interrupted him. I said I was never in such a good humor when I was quite unknown. I complained to him of being appallingly hungry, of tragic dreams of getting food to eat, but of never having the satisfaction of dreaming that I was actually eating. Last night I did taste bread and butter. He laughed. "I assumed," he said, "that you would be guided by your common sense and that you would have had more confidence in your father's judgment which you know is so sound, than in your own futile wishes. For lunch we will have Wild Roll, shepherd's pie, fresh baked soda-bread, hot milk treacle, pudding, nuts, raisins, and cake. After that we will turn in for a sleep, and we will be called at 3:45, when we will reach out again from the bunks and have doughnuts and sweets. We will get up then and have big cups of tea, and fresh cakes and chocolate creams. Dinner will be at six, and we will have thick soup, roast beef and Yorkshire pudding, cauliflower, peas, asparagus, plum pudding, fruit, apple pie with thick cream, scones and butter, port wine, nuts, and almonds and raisins."

He raised his forefinger. "These seemingly trivial matters may often bring success, honor, and wealth, or, on the other hand, disgrace. At midnight we will have a really big meal, just before we go to bed. There will be melon, grilled trout and butter sauce, roast chicken with plenty of livers, and a proper salad with eggs and very thick dressing, green peas and new potatoes, a saddle of mutton, fried suet pudding, peaches à la Melba, egg curry, plum pudding and sauce, celery, fruit, nuts, port wine, milk, and cocoa. Then we will go to bed and sleep until breakfast. We will have chocolate and biscuits under our pillows, and if we want anything to eat during the night we will just have to get it! Trust no one! Keep your medicines! Go to bed early! Do not catch cold! Perspire a little every morning! Be careful in your diet! Good night!"

I spent my life with my grandfather. The dangers I did know were preferable to those I did not know.

By the painful process of forcing my eyelids apart with my fingers I was able to see a little, but the pain was severe. I endured six hours of agony, ending in a good long sleep, from which I awoke much refreshed. By midnight I was walking to the rookery, where I had great fun with the birds.

CUPID & PSYCHE

for Sherril & David

Psyche

I am prepared to hear these
numbers, and steadfastly
investigate the indistinct part,
my so called wings
mothballed over with sacred
or theoretical crud.
Is the material likely to breed
two fair creatures, couched
side by side
or will many small disgraceful
gestures die in its
crystallizations? I
was looking for you.
I could have been there myself.

Hers

I'll embrace my inclination
a soft set up
torn
thoroughly blue silver white
a hard breathing
winged devouring approaching
thinking
I was in my eyes

Cupid

A lover who is detected
breeding flowers in her brain
whom he sought
abandoning his life
which pleasures enjoy in his place
and afterwards cause him
to suffer little distinctly
letting the warm error return
home welcomed with foolish
thunder and lightning

His

I'll embrace my inclination
a soft set up
torn
thoroughly blue silver white
a hard breathing
winged devouring approaching
thinking
I was in my eyes

Pleasure

Pleasure is never a mystery.
Witnesses acknowledge a mutual
admiration underneath
a banner of usefulness,
company, recent vows
enjoying a little view.
I can't remember what I saw
before I told you
what I thought was there:
persuasive beauty muffled in
established tendernesses
which neither had any idea
what or who—finally questions
to leave alone.

Alone

leave to questions
finally—who, or what
idea either had, or neither,
which tendernesses
established and muffled.
There was thought. I,
what you told me before
I saw what I remember:
a view. Enjoying little,
vows, recent company,
usefulness,
admiration acknowledged,
witnessed pleasure.

Blood

Two can blush in a fit of abstraction,
and not with the blood of their
ancestors either. This alteration
may be supported by the authority
of some shadowy window open at night
as one drives one's tight fitting
desires by. The hook may not be seen.
Comical untrodden syntax
tucked away in a three hour
phonecall or headache.
Put what you like on the table,
the gardener will never delight
flowers that are both
believable and replaceable.

Thought

A shadowy thought tight rooted
to the forehead over hours
and hours oozing by fabulous
and irrational intelligent beings
who sometimes sing in a manner
worthy of inclination and who
merely twitter at others,
choosing coarser praises:
Honor to the unshorn!
and the luxury
they ride on, sinking
or rising as the forehead
suffers to be kissed.

Flattery

It is the custom of mankind
to abstract Beauty and then sleep
in the ashes of her ill repute.
A few, sad, last grey hairs
then fur and claws
arise and grow, and to think
is to be full of sorrow,
the body merely
one side of the equation.
But a new Love pines
behind the window, and how great
is the encouragement the world
gives the lover, the whole body
evenly smooth in front
of a green arras
wrinkled at the bottom

HOW TO IMPROVE

for Barrett Watten

Into

The utility is certain. Were it not, the present could not chase the greatest ultimate.

So much the most casual will readily learn. Each has a residence, in a jumble of individuality. And personality, the peasant of motion, aloof, unmoved, the effect of sentimental song. Imagine the wall, changed unto mind!

Human personalities for their own sakes can become so vigorous that *fair & radiant maidens* nearly always are creatures of the same defunct charm over years of fashion.

The *moron* has now become all mass. Born, come to maturity, gone old, dead, resurrected but to die again, restored, killed, living on, maimed, rejuvenated, betrayed, married, mutilated, detoxified, separated. Cities build emphasis. Soothe the ears, move the tears to a can. Hundreds of thousands accurately expressing the elements.

But, for all this, sadly abused. The *thing* under a weary, weary burden, bent and broken. The vitality which so fatigues, the slave with few lives. He has to get along with vague impressions of half of some things at all. *Retire*, unnecessarily and often. The average place. The bad taste of teeth. The man wears a broad grin to keep them.

You, however, are important enough for a separate number (no. 82).

A pill will correct the true student overnight. His is the aggressive swallow. It may tell.

Single Words

Most users mean little, it's true. The enormous source seems a trifle. Some illustrations get compared with existence, which must in time grow smaller. The twentieth century uses the average. The end.

The exact person ought to continue. Certainly, no one can afford to stop. A person's experience must contain several meanings, or he cannot be careful.

Sound requires any speaker to know sound. *Improve, enlarge.* Suppose a basis:

Life is a happier wish
than to be laid.
A cool syringa's shade
or wavy willow; the dragon,
content of purple crest
and filmy indifference;
the water-lily's golden
overlook—
What I am in
believes me, who will live forever
and drop dead into the river!
God pardon fancy things!

The fundamental importance here cannot be discounted. If not available, consult the first opportunity. The thing is to unfamiliar any clear understanding that has preceded the moment.

Be sure that you are aware of the shades. *Thou art* old. *Be* aloft, again & again. Perform, instead of merely washing your hands. *Awake* is enough, and wonders why it is ever omitted from the essential. Superseded, *swoon* largely by, *faint away*, a distinct addition, possibly *steadfast*.

The world is too late.
Getting our powers
we see in.
We have given our hearts away!
Solid boon!
The hours are gathered
like this tune.
It moves not the pleasant lea.

Suppose we examine a great deal of care. First, its definition: a state of being. Splendid. 1) Emitted or reflected. 2) Used. The *splendor* of *rare* disregard. *Accuracy* applies to star. And a star shines with accuracy. We learn through meaning to *shine*. Splendid. A distinct gain.

Turning, we are stuck. We notice our ears are trained. Soft harmonies of deeptoned, nevertheless quiet, repeated questions suited to the context enrage the attention. It is no good. Every thing uses any music to make the use of us sound so precise. Submerge valuable connotations. If they survive, they have their duties.

Notice the remarkable loss of vividness known as a blanket. It includes all degrees of night. Lost, idealized. Our own eyes should discern we can't improve unerringly.

Abandoning *splendor*, it can be seen. Figurative fundamental sense without implications of appearance. A man in armor is hardly furnished tastefully with the best. He reads and hopes. He may not have a single shining thing within. Yet he may, robed in satins and the usual sense, speak of various meanings, a genuine part of our process.

Improving may appear tedious, and, a great many times, monotonous, an exacted platitude. It rumbles somewhat, rather loose in its application. Most of the time goes by.

Conference

People yield themselves. They hunger, and lack. You must search out the individuals. Step aside from conversations, sermons. Grasp the stranger and look straight in at this moment. Do you feel ease? Cold? Some denizens boast that they know their "names." John, Bob, Jim is a walking average menu. You are in no danger from one another.

> Winter wind,
> thou art not
> my tooth.

Some rather startling things are queer and grotesquely illogical. It is a universal habit to skip over indefinite mental processes. Just indulge, and be wrong. The next time you are likely to think the same way. Until, at last, to be associated inseparably with *noisome*. Eyes, nose, even the lines about the mouth are a shock to push you along to your ultimate misunderstanding.

> Autumn wastes each day.
> The sky stirs the cold blue rope.
> I have tied
> the barbarians to my house.
> I'll hoe myself,
> and from my dinner plate
> arm the brook!

Easy to sense the course.
Hard to compel the drift of joy.
In the deepest decline
the leafiest will conquers its age.
And praise and blame to youth.
Though autumn is on my failings,
I shall never weary of my pillow.

The first time you meet the pigs in their pen, the proximity looks as though it means "full of you, disinclined to look." Think, grunting and squealing, and pass by. You may even be so far gone you cast a cold eye. Then you notice a new connection: "The noisome odor of the slaughterhouse." A brief consultation will put you right again, and show you the means, and furthermore, the kinship.

Verify your present, then. Pick out distinct individuals and see them. (Not as *case, take*, etc., but purely *as*.) You have a surprise in store. You are an extraordinary human being.

Pretty escape
    the other day
        you fled away
I have since caught you
        flying   Stars
                                pouring
                     osiers
        Kisses here   devouring
Never   lips there
  full
soon
  loves   Desert
                   keeping
    And   my desires safe
      aught
        should be
   your servant
      my saint

Room

Writing is a room, a method of dilating the pupils. Horace speaks: "Listen. I have a surface. Every day, at least. Then I sentence words to various shades of meaning. Day after day I am looking at that picked garden. Amaranthine glory of her leonine dignity sat gravely on the gypsying hinterlands."

You can verify your so-and-so. You can merely know how to use it. Let it go at that. We can stop. We haven't learned at all, technical, specialized. Equal in value with the royal background.

> I might have known.
> The immaculate pencil.
> The inexcusable, comma.
> Ritual lives of endless objects.

Define your own scorn. Redden, endless, extravagant. Couch upon the bed, lake, beast. Look at what you can. Try to avoid preceding today. Follow splendor about. It does shine figuratively with a magnificence firmly between its teeth.

The Ancestry

A man's a man and the past. Develop a spare, or don't be surprised to discover you haven't walked in primly. Take it on faith: it is somehow interesting to manage to use the door. Compare the value of belief with the actual widespread experience of fate, a power that flowed in your mouth before you began to exert your influence. Imagine the tortured "holiday" of having food be kept in myth, just beyond more vivid dexterity.

Old lights are in the ground today. They appertain to you, whether you swallow the earth, or provoke the lord in the pit.

> Sweet in her dull green flower
> beauty slumbers, a lulled
> sigh lumbering through her air.
>
> Onward to my fatal wings.

Another gone! Heaven's blank cheque
has bounced again.
With nightly music the spheres
sweep the splendid years
under the rug.
Birds call up the forest,
intelligible rocks echo their alarm.

Shakespeare is universally assumed the world's greatest uncle. So it is impossible to read Shakespeare. Large numbers of intelligent-looking students serve obsolete basilisks. They find themselves clarifying the descriptions. Smiling like milk dropping into easy chairs. Vinegar is nearer what we want, sharp, sour, eager boycott, veto, sinister lariat sensing the literal.

The paint is always peeling
from common sense.
The men are shaved smooth
as putting greens
and the sky's blue smoke
appears by its own appointment.

Kinsmen

If ancestors, they are innumerable. Large groups of boasting families. The kinsmen are *profane, fanatic* blood brothers. Numbers separate; one sister goes to India, a brother to Iceland, but at some far time, they come to the same land, and meet. They marry, and spend the *week-end* in front of the *looking-glass*, as fully recognized as the postman in his doublets.

The brain falls open to the story, dog-eared and looking for a good time. Rhymes with ice, and slips on the trail of its own firm footsteps. The brain can be a *manacle*. The Romans slapped their slaves' minds. But then, they had large families.

Hard study finds the rocks before sense has any idea stretching. Confusing elements are repeated until the project is thrown across the familiar and ends up at a careless day nursery where two or three children are playing tag and being rewarded with gentle vocal chisels.

The duke was playing the phonograph. To provoke logic, he declared biology an aberration. But run your hand across it. Genealogy decides nothing; guesses hit the mark, generous vocatives occur, inducing conduct, and concurring with the benediction. Simply sit, out of thought's way.

> Lightly I tricked the Clouds
> to gather the sober
> coloring of an eye.
> I have kept my watch.

> The human heart,
> thanks to its human,
> gets tough
> with the meanest flower.

Combination

Pairs are of little use unless they are continually one another. The child learning to talk hardly waits. He knows half a dozen places. His chance to get them straight becomes inevitably confused in the student's mind. Crude combinations develop and they grow into finished statements.

Intelligence now begun. You have hours and minutes. Your answers will be familiar to you.

cold _____		best _____	
high _____		sharp _____	
east _____		soft _____	
wet _____		strong _____	
girl _____		drunk _____	
night _____		dark _____	
slow _____		sweet _____	
major _____		enemy _____	

Very well, *objective* and *subjective*. You learn the one, and you might well be the other. The association will be complimentary. The one will defy and vivify the other. It feels like the zenith, nadir. Notice the number of opaque, orthodox verticals. Read the newspapers, study the walls.

Love, like pity, consumes *verse*. The *costume* of the teacher is the opposite of *healthy*. The *customer* should lay loose in the *piazza*. Furthermore, *sarcasm* is later than it would like to *suppose*. If the *continual* affects your allusions, it is customary to call a *halt*.

When the person has been speaking for years, it is the quite possible of which he is quite aware. Gait, gate. Right, wrong. Never for a moment does he submit. His one world completely overlaps the others and hides them. This increases his task. It becomes impossible.

Nice Try

(1) Kneeling is a gesture. (2) He said he would never consider the menace again. (3) He used the ax against the shed. (4) Ask him where he thinks he's going. (5) The gloom of the cemetery was clearly visible. (6) The document was destroyed.

The world does a great many things. *Things* is one. We saw *splendor* at the beginning. It is appalling that the record of it does not reinvent this happy notion. It has been used, and the literal act has not returned; though it be followed by an Amen! and Lo! attention is too colorless to strike.

Students wonder at the deeper meaning the dictionary's colder analysis gives us. It is much like the name of a person we know. Thus, *Virginia* may be a deeply personal lass happily named *Virginia*, a blithely emotional loveable term. A great help.

Can you imagine tantalizing a thirsty man with a beaker of H_2O? His agony would be trebled by the mere sound. A cup of cold water is due to the instant commotion, the mastery of words.

> I have thinned an airy site
> hungrier than rain can lay
> whims like sores on years fleeing.
>
> I am not one hundred percent
> the ladder of death
> and willingly digest the fields
> and the stinging populace.

Chew superbly, and,
if queasy, cling
to the flying mane.

Taken in sensible doses, most tonics are likely to result in the stupor of inebriate self-pronunciation. Any passage of Shakespeare avoids Shakespeare's thoughts, even though you yourself may have taken Shakespeare's word for it. The cats meow.

BEFORE WATER

The clear sentence the world ends
The clear sound the water made
Once the noise vocabulary
The sentence is an obstacle to noise
Ponderous forethought enables the sound to read its own mind
Clever of the world to rise crest fall white noise
Edit the end once again
Dries clear and won't give birth
Blue over once one more noise
Hear it say itself to what I see
Water before the sound until the sound fills
The world end the sentence ends
One sense to a vocabulary
Each time of course the sentence completes
I make the noise of vocabulary
After it was a sentence it's a sound
Water roll sense make blue
Do one to the end
The clear blue birth of green
Touching itself the sentence learns its loop
The end makes birth once
Blue course no noise in this sentence
No noise in this sentence
The sentence goes over itself
Ponderous water the end of noise
Leaning over each death edge complete
Blue and noise at each edge of the sound
The sense against the water
The sentence ends when made
While it's before through to when I hear it
Vocabulary enables forethought to end
Roll over watery noise the sentence says to
Blue water at the sense's edge
This sentence learned to roll over
It's up to blue to say
Each vocabulary contains its own blue
The clearer the world the nearer the edge
I make my sense to the end

Green water learns to dry
Each edge of the water
Every once it's over
To the edge to the end no noise
To the end of noise the mind occurs once falls water
I touch the water's clever noise
I only think of this each time
The sentence starts to contain water and spills
This water was once a sentence
White water touching blue water
Each sentence is complete
Each sentence is the same
The same sounds give birth to the same sentence nearer the end
Each sentence completes the world
Sound ties thought to itself
The thought of the death of thought gives mind its edge
Clear thought nearly noise
The sentence made clever death noise
Blue makes sense once
Watery noise over the water
The world makes sense once a sentence
Water is made of thought
The world is blue
A loop no noise of the completed edge
Water makes blue make white
I made each time line up
I read my own blue
A loop around was or will be
I hear noise make sense
The end of the noise the edge of the sentence
Each ponderous birth of vocabulary rolls in
Do it once
Does this noise completely end the world
The senses fall to white noise loops
The sentence is a line of water in order to read my mind through once
The sentence in a noise of falling order green extent
Once it's done the world dries
I made death green only to think
The world is made of sentences
White time lines the sense with noise

There was no vocabulary in the water
I edit sense
The water rises in the middle to end the sentence
I learned to read before I heard a sound
See it say water
The noise of it, water of it
The clear blue sea is just noise
I made a sound, it made a noise
It goes and went dry
Each sentence completes the thought that tells it where to start
I start the sea
Once a sound occurs it's over
I is a sound that occurs again and again to the same water
Green once again
Before I end thought I end
The sentence makes itself
Forethought touches water before water extends the sense
What's the sense of thinking every thought
I say to see the water
I never think I'm the same as thought
Time is lined up noise
Blue or lined green
Blue is complete sense
The noise of thought occurs to make thought ponderous
Noise is the same difference as water and thought
Every sense each time
Loop the time against death
The middle of the sentence never ends
The middle of the same noise makes a different sense
The world on edge rolls its own water
I'm here to make noise make sense
I will only sense completed time once
Blue makes its sound sound blue
Once it's a sentence it's never the same
The shape of the sentence is clear beyond the water
It is the end of itself
Roll the sentence over the edge
This loop over this loop
Toward water while in the sentence
The sound water

Green for mind, water for noise
Where to leave the water's edge
Water to the edge of each sentence
The world learns to end
There is no water there
White says itself
Do I learn sound
See against sentences
The mind okays the noise, the water pushes the mind away
Sentences are shape, the world is end
White spill no world
I same I think water I water
Thought extends throughout the sentence
Blue start up edge over makes this sound a noise away
A full sentence complete with water
Blue each time or green every same time
Nowhere in the sentence is there a noise for water
Is it or isn't it what it says
The same thought the same time as the same thing
Sentence says so sound may go
Loose blue water or I thought it
I'm a shape I shape
There is more thought than time, more vocabulary than water
Thought is clear and clearly not water
Each edge marks where two senses end
No time before this thought to think it
The noise of the time before
By the middle of the sound the sentence was here
Water in the same sense as a broken line of noise never ends
The world ends what I think extends beyond the sentence
Blue starts with no time
Born blue on the only edge
Never once or here again
Noise touching the sentence to pound it to water
Now the world starts completely over
See blue say noise
Mind or water in order
No because of noise
My mind's made up
One sentence makes the world

In here it's there out here
One and think again to say it
Send the sound to the end of the line
More time each time
I shape the loop with vocabulary that enables noise to crest
The white line never stays white
Think one of the sounds
Each is the same as the edge and disappears
I say blue I see blue
Sound on edge makes the sentence see itself
I hear the sound while it's over
Nowhere until it appears
A noise says to hear
Blue and again it's water
Looped noise vocabulary more than noise can learn to see
Touch before and water after
It's the end that makes birth violent
Thought as sound of itself
The noise learns to be water in time to roll white words into the
    sentence
Vocabulary was always the same as noise
Once it was there and now it's never a sound outside
The sentence stands in the middle of the water
The color of the water the sound of the sentence
Each shape starts all over itself
Blue nowhere outside of noise
Green at the same time it's said
I touch each sentence to the thought of what I hear
The blue line means water, the noise means blue
This sentence is full up
Death gives blue noise out there
The water starts to rise
A sound of it
Blue
Ponderous completely filled in thought ends before
Wrinkled water behaves itself
The sound of water ends at once
Once I'm here I see lines
Noises think the same thing
Mind thought the noise mind

Even where it happens it ends
Once in and gone
Water extends blue across the looped noise
I see uncovered blue as a noise
A sentence across the end of all it can think
One sentence to the edge of green without more green
Sense is a loop of sense once it's thought
End spills dry to here or noise
Another white and the same white
A different sentence goes across the sentence
The water completes the sounds
It's gone between the sound and where it is
The completed spill
Time goes as ready sense
Once and not
Went in
Loops each noise against the mind I see in
Complete thought includes a separate vocabulary for each sound
All the water spilled in one sentence
No more than noise with an edge
Touched no other than the same thing
Water coming in once I shape what it says
The same things complete a different world
Green and blue or see into it
Time a variation of one
Time before the end of the sentence to say
Each noise enables itself to go away
It's over to have a shape
Thought against vocabulary against sense through to the end
World against itself as water
I can only hear the same sound
A green thought against the completed world
I as a noise it can think
The sea is nearly never ready to contain water
As the thing sounds I read the same thought
Each complete sentence says time will end
I see it as it falls away
One is a loop
A complete sentence invites the world to be outside
No sound inside shape

Thought has no choice between water and thought
The world occurs against what the sense of it enables the sentence to
    say
I fall is the edge
A sentence is here and over
No blue, no green, no water, itself complete
A sentence threw the water away
Say it through it
It took here to think more sound
Think once in and edge
Tied itself across what was said
I think a sentence while it starts
Inside the covered sound
Leave the water at birth
I see it until it's water
I can't think again
Tell the water where to start
I see around the sound
Sound in the same sense as birth makes sense
The sentence goes back to where it came from
Green through itself
The noise varies itself to make me hear the same thing it said
Time once established goes away
Such shape as the sentence takes away from the world
Touch sense to water
The water rolls as before water
The water sounds okay
The noise crosses the sentence
I'm ready to see
It's water again

MY ONE VOICE

At the sound of my voice
I spoke and, egged on
By the discrepancy, wrote
The rest out as poetry.

Read the books, duets
From nowhere say they speak;
Why not let them. Inhabited stares
Leave trees in rearview mirrors.

I came from a neutral point
In space, far from the inside
Of any one head. O say can I
Still see the tabula rasa outshining

That rosy dawn on the near side
Of the genetic code. Doubt,
Thy name is certainty. Generations
Of recordings of the sunrise

Picture the light until the page
Is white and I predict
The present, hearing a future
In the syllables' erasing day.

TRAINEE

The language has us by the throat,
Scorched utensils in a grid. Trained
Tracks, right of way, light
Of day. Enraged bodies whistle by
Cold soot, skipping space entirely.

Letters are so dense it's convenient
To stop listening. Religious
Seduction scenarios replace
The melancholy human voice,
Its perfected products, trick photos.

Say I say sky, say the city
Of San Francisco sits beneath that.
Have you ever seen a school fence?
A sun set? Fields of speech
The anatomizing phonemes bark at.

A machine shop? In the light
Of the correct time, steel beams
Lift a low stone fog. Tires sing
On freeways that guard the views
From distressed housing.

Convinced condensed devices are at home
In our words. Not to be confused
With us or use. Remove
The caressed blossom, the rug's still
Brand new, a vacuum.

BONDING

Speech makes a show of force,
A self-proclaimed surplus
Wandering outwards. We listen
Blindly, devoted to the incoming

Likeness. Rhyme charms,
But the charm fades. The units
Make a clicking noise
Impossible to mask.

Some stick together
In after the fact
Probability, but the film
Can break anywhere. Any face

Registers the odds.
Matter animates
The great song, weeping
At the bottom of the well.

Feeling one's place
Shift, feet support
A random weight. The planet
Is coated with rock,

Machines, candy. The tongue
Is in the mouth.
The moon in the sky
Is more than a coincidence.

DAYS

One word is next
To another, an excess
Of localism, solidarity, and
Vive la differance shouted
Down crowded column inches.
Each voice singled out
By ages of technique.

In fact you don't
Live a life one
Day at a time.
Some days you skip,
Come back to them
Later, others never occur.
These locations are not
Even up for grabs,
Cause no comment.

TO BAUDELAIRE

The head is the body's lair.
It may be slightly in front.
Milking these separations,
Words answer the immortal need

For intoxicating monotony. The body
Is the mind's sieve.
Beloved grief, water drips
From a block of red ice

Onto a perfumed paradise
Lost in the obsessive embrace
Of reader and writer. Superb haloes
Hang from the heads

Of naked slaves whipping themselves.
A new world is required
To stomach the images
Floating on the headless

Torso of the old.
"I was surprised to find myself
Staring at an empty hole.
I ordered flowers."

ROOM

The words mention themselves.
They are literally true.
Every minute another circle
Meets itself halfway.

The locker locks
From the inside. I
Is an extensive pun
Born of this confinement,

The echoes crossing
North America, the room.
The ear hears in no time.
On the street, machines

Reveal the thought
Of non-machines. These
Objects have the right
To remain silent.

The pen wrestles with
The hand by the light
Of an open door. Things
Are their real size.

CHINA

We live on the third world from the sun. Number three. Nobody tells
us what to do.

The people who taught us to count were being very kind.

It's always time to leave.

If it rains, you either have your umbrella or you don't.

The wind blows your hat off.

The sun rises also.

I'd rather the stars didn't describe us to each other; I'd rather we do it
for ourselves.

Run in front of your shadow.

A sister who points to the sky at least once a decade is a good sister.

The landscape is motorized.

The train takes you where it goes.

Bridges among water.

Folks straggling along vast stretches of concrete, heading into the plane.

Don't forget what your hat and shoes will look like when you are nowhere to be found.

Coats in the window hung up on hooks; question marks where the heads would normally be.

Even the words floating in air make blue shadows.

If it tastes good we eat it.

The leaves are falling. Point things out.

Pick up the right things.

Hey guess what? What? *I've learned how to talk.* Great.

The person whose head was incomplete burst into tears.

As it fell, what could the doll do? Nothing.

Go to sleep.

You look great in shorts. And the flag looks great too.

Everyone enjoyed the explosions.

Time to wake up.

But better get used to dreams too.

I

I AM OFTEN CONSCIOUS, but rain is now visibly falling. It almost combines to be one thing, but here I am again. Though he dreamed he was awake, it was a mistake he would only make at a time like that. There are memories, but I am not that person.

An inspected geography leans in with the landscape's repetitions. He lived here, under the assumptions. The hill suddenly vanished, proving him right. I was left holding the bag. I peered into it.

The ground was approaching fast. It was a side of himself he rarely showed. The car's tracks disappeared in the middle of the road. The dialog with objects is becoming more strained. Both sides gather their forces. Clouds enlarge. The wind picks up. He held onto the side of the barn by his fingertips.

The little eye muscles flicked the pictures happily from side to side. The buildings, the sky were delighted. They broke into capital letters. A cloud of minute degrees idealizes itself, until I see what I thought. Who the world is, can tell by my language. He took a scissors and cut out a quarter of the record.

The lids of known things, dissolved behind the scenes. In place of remarks, read mournful silence. Each second the features repeat. These hills are the same ones they are. The past will contain the future. I found that I had put my shoes on backwards. I faced the other way. By the time he got back there, he had forgotten the way back. He was back home, out back. Audibly, it was centuries collapsing.

The letters of the week are like the days in the words. The mind fills with what's left. One thought connects with another, until by paying attention I ran like a clock. The earth revolves quickly. He displayed his scars.

I name the things after the words that sponsor them. He normally knew little of the depths below daily consciousness, except for what the shifting weights and tones of the immediate senses never fail to lay out over long periods drifting across the whole thing. I'm afraid I didn't catch . . . He fell off a log.

· ·

Everybody gets a biography. Pinholes effect the maximum registration. Vocabularies set up camp of a blurred, running, bloody map. Now they write the lyrics out so I'll know what the song is talking about. Faces choosing their type, and vice versa. Schoolboy torn in half by book. An italicized *I* staggers down the street, making its demands known to the traffic.

As simple as starting at infinity and ending in drab, glum haste, missing the whole boat. But he could never see that the days performed any useful function, taken separately. It's a question of nerve, learning to forget just in time. And there is the damp corner where the story is kept. He's in there, too, agonizing over won-lost records. It's a confusion, some doorway wanted out of the seasons. Captured by the first thing I hear, I think a difference, but simply was, finally. A splendid personal view accessible after years of filtering. Black and white sunlight added to the inventory. Print on enduring paper, etc. Test of time to withstand test of time.

Backlog of outtakes, smiles, folding matchbooks. Two thousand year old empire in eight year old brain. No beginning. A logging road, I was there, it was gone. Daylight washes sentiment out onto the road. It says what it is. He meant to say, or dreamt to blend, bend. Vibrations breaking colors buzz away. The earth grows more literal each year.

In a dream a piece of writing is a raised surface, one word standing for another on the lower level. One element is substituted for another via the simple authority of say so, being there. The distance traversed is charming, extravagant. Moustache reads as the eyebrows of a woman in flannel, a distant relation, dancing. He heard the voice stop muttering and it was replaced by his own, booming instructions down to the valley below. Smoke curls up from chimneys throughout the charming Swiss village of Denkmittel.

He heard the music and stood up. Played at appropriate speed, incurable motion out the window. The names are maintained to prevent accumulations of self-esteem from crashing too harmlessly into private abysses. As if hearing were a perfection of air perpetrated among rivals, sets of teeth, synonyms, sentence structure, ruptured blood vessels. He held on, in advance. Night fell, and I lived through that, too, expressing the expressible in terms of the expressed. On good terms with neighbors, dependable, daily, there, smiles, and is currently reading and writing this sentence.

ONCE UPON A TIME, THERE was a bb in a boxcar. Miles, extended; physical earth, the. I inhale the fragrance myself and know it and like it. The view is inscribed onto a white disk, then seen.

A foreground of blank stress competes. Personal impressions are sung to sleep across a roaring gorge, eaten by subvocalic automatism. The released noise opens, fortune cookies speading to strangers on intimate terms. The waves rose, wet, green.

The door is heroically small and tight. Vivid memoirs skid on the sidewalk, alive, a weight. I assure you I am the body in quesion. The cat chases the mouse into his hole, bangs against the wall.

Voices shade and light my face. Mica sparkles, the infant's lit up features mimicking. Pages fall off the calendar and fill the house, which finally bursts. It's not possible to get any of the characters, once introduced, off the stage. He parted his hair in the gathering realism.

Each singer sings the song exactly as he learned it. Speech is the twin of my vision. He stood on the porch and outlined the steps. The voice rose, denoting an uphill battle. The torchlit procession was bound by infinite space.

The eye is a tool, the sky an exercise in positive thinking. The camera closes in on horses, heroes, and succulents. Scenery has its price, rolling over. Trained actors deliver off the cuff eulogies to the shattered euphemism. What was for lunch is still a mystery. It's around here somewhere.

There are two types of story: something happens, or it doesn't have to. To register a change of state, water freezes, explorers bob on isolate floes. Taste deranges its choices. Perceptibility walks in backwards, disappears into the chair. At the end of the tale, the robot turns out to be made of flesh and blood.

He saw ahead in time as far as his fingertips. They were out there, a moral, pyrrhic, victory. The ocean pounded the shore, the connoisseur's tuneless grave. It could have been anything, but finally it was his, a white file cabinet. The log burned with a simple virtuosity, as fast as he could see.

At a certain point, I am an ass and need to be kissed. In the light of a vertical drop of years, psychology chafes the categories, cars going by, cold, orange, smoke, October, Sunday. Grammar plus person, parsed from inside, split up into ones. They got married, publicly smashing the hourglass. The mind is whole and undivided, the sound a continuous stream, all Cretans are liars. His ears are long. They make love.

Breathless accounts of the decisive moment blurred, multiplied. Hen's teeth in a hailstorm, Judy Garland in Kansas. Perhaps you could jettison the thought and live for the sound. Gorgeous panoply stares through, blue stars in white noise. A spiritual calling, shooting the mirror out from under the page. Nature abhors a vacuum.

Inside the box was a cubic mile of air, time to breathe, and marks on the ruler. I know, I was there. Repetitious need frames list. Opens mouth to divert dream posse. Real-life critic takes stand on taking up room. Sentence points out consciouness depot. But reader reading, same as matter, conclusive. And so we draw the curtain.

Some realists get smashed down at Land's End. The force of the cars stands dreamily in the steady offshore wind. Goddesses, cards, numbers hold the scene up for introspection. But nobody is there to listen as the satire confesses. Nostalgia for street signs with dew on them. A new generation of leaves left for the redecorated front.

A voice ricochets off the rocks next to my ear. Wordless vistas bulge out of memory, enormous, pressing to transmute. My ankle bends the cause of my slightest wish. Pleasure in the design and a witless consent as the mind is left chained to the high rocks of the mountain. My page makes love, and he can't read.

The sentence rives and gives birth to itself. I can say this happening. Being born works like a charm. An amulet of sound worn round the neck. The bend in the river, where it starts talking. The enraptured artist ate the terrified neurotic. The body, water, falls, drops, drowns, appearance undoes itself. The broken code recedes before my prophetic screams. The letters represent ancient journeys, which continue.

The goddess of the tunnel of love is the top of the water. The tickets are printed on thick red paper. Doors gotten through at a glance, instantaneous duration. The surface is alive, punctuated by skirts and pants, shoes, electric hums. The glamor is not in the names, but the bodies.

There's an increasing pressure to identify with history, 14 lbs per square inch. People carry weights, and enforce continuity. The headlines display Brownian motion, while editorials preach a thick skin. Cranks go to the wrong country, climb Alps, shout down the glories of light to a world of doghouses. Heidi comes down to the city, and marries Hitler, just in from the suburbs.

Eventually, they filled in the hole, composed two epics, memorized the beat, and wrote down what was left. The city was rebuilt as scattered hamlets. Language sank into the ground. Ideas became too highly charged to be put into practice. Laughter shared with the opposite sex was effeminate, brazen. Walking down the road, hand in hand, Babar and Celeste are Daddy and Mommy. They each wear a crown.

Night falls, the tv comes on. The Lone Ranger rears into the dark sky. The episodes are on an equal footing, day after day. Premise, delay, conclusion, dinner. The exits are never convenient. The wolf misses a curve, plows through the mountains.

A voice calls out from the natural theater as the movie is slipping under my fingertips. Running time pulsing by heart. Underlying the sound, a mixture of sand, ships' hulls, crustaceous debris. It was as if one wasn't in control of the environment. Hundreds of us watched the film, a badly mutilated print of Clark Gable and Jean Harlow. Relentless desire animated the frames.

Here is a memory of itself. He looked through the hole in the middle of the record. One side is the eagle, the other the snake. Together they're worth about 2 cents. Sparkles of day and dusk, broad muscular fields bypass the fovea. Meaning spread and blew.

If darkness is speech, and hearing lightens it up a bit, still, the shapes are on the outside. I'm not walking around inside my head, nor are you. We might have made beautiful splashes of silver nitrate in some mind's eye. Frozen solid, the cold is to be taken personally? Individual hills of ice? Dissolved belle-lettristic prose of the saber-toothed tiger? Reason is an emotion so volatile it can't be moved.

Language is what is told. The locus classicus turns out to be where they dump old cars. An endless line of visitors are told in turn that time is up. A few craned necks spotted the beast in the jungle.

The body writes its flowing loops, hopes, disappears. Replaceable parts stare at the dividing line, scuff shoes, dream dreams, name names. Senses submit their ratios. The blocks are regular, the city a shapeless threat to the rewards it holds hundreds of feet above its streets. Yellow sunlight filters down onto my grandparents learning English in a green, smoky landscape.

Large trees are loaded onto old railway cars. In that country the last days glisten, reflect watery sun up into the features of my grandfather I didn't escape. Bygones do not let bygones be bygones. Masters in search of more slaves. The dead wood formed a rude retort.

Why is today different from all other days? A very loud wind believes this question deserves flapping and rattling metal. Large tough maple leaves want to happen all at once. I prefer to string it out in the sunlight, the ground doing conscious battle with what I say. In honor of the place, people differ. Porous border ballads, to be sung anywhere.

Private corners resist, trap dust, speak in tongues. Stone-age button-pushers film the tribe that lives under the billboards, making love by kinship degrees. There may have been an unbroken body beneath the words, now speak. The narrowing circle of light swallows Bugs Bunny, looking over his shoulder and chewing on a carrot.

The wave reared up, a lofty allegory made entirely of water. Time went the wrong way down a dead-end street to a paradise at the foot of the view. The principle of recurrence allows me to see the sky. Infinite regress soothed the familiar irony of his doubt. It crashed on the sand.

The day of judgement was at birth. These climaxes are subjective. The hero stood still and flexed his fame, glared in the light of his glowing one-way ticket, a serpentine seduction. One per universe, the first person came and went. Small houses of snow turn on the news.

> Each second is the same,
> yet art is never a science.
> If you can't remember her name,
> she's not your fiancée.

Staring the prompter in the face, does nothing till name is pronounced by visible elements, takes notes, years. Succeeds. Wildest dreams. Anything he said kept talking. The cut flowers drank from their stems. The page remained full of writing. There are ways to do this, all physical.

The sky was grey, and tiers of dripping leaves cracked the light apart. The words were gray, producing approximations of the places we'll be seen, stated, carrying bombastic visas as our eyes raise storms in the collapsible theaters clumped around the solid vowels. Topside, there was constant snow of torn-up calendar pages along streets miles long. I was round, and couldn't define the vine I dangled from. Sex required separation, shy fractions. The movies appealed for the opposite reason. My fate is to be translated into words and set down by hand on paper that remembers its untutored spring in the air moved by gusts of varying temperatures, squalls, and defects also, that were to be made good by obsessive roots forging themselves out of hard-packed dirt.

THE UNRULY CHILD

There is a company called Marathon Oil, mother,
Very far away and very big and, again, very
Desirable. Who isn't? Back connecting pure dots,
Fleecy intelligence lapped in explanatory sound
The faces make difficult.

Learn the language.
That beautiful tongue-in-cheek hostage situation:
My mind, up close, in pjs, and I use it.
Wanting to fuck an abstraction nine times in a row,
Continuous melismata, don't stop, don't stop, no name, no picture.

There is a series of solids, mother,
Called people, who rise to the transparent obtainable
Solo windows, mornings, afternoons,
And there are military operations called
Operation Patio, Operation Menu.

It is the individuals who finally get the feel of the tenses.
So that it may snow, has to snow on the muddy corpse.
There is a boundary, mother, very far away and very
Continuous, broken, to interrogate civilians, the self,
The text, networks of viewers found wanting a new way
To cook chicken, why not?, to kill while falling asleep.
There is the one language not called money, and the other not called
    explosions.

SEDUCED BY ANALOGY

First sentence: *Her cheap perfume*
Caused cancer in the White House late last night.
With *afford, agree* and *arrange*, use the infinitive.
I can't agree to die. With *practice*,
Imagine, and *resist*, use the gerund. *I practice to live*
Is wrong. Specify. "We're got to nuke 'em, Henry."
Second sentence: *Inside the box is plutonium.*
The concept degrades, explodes,
Goes all the way, in legal parlance.

"I can't stop. Stop. I can't stop myself."
First sentence: *She is a woman who has read*
Powers of Desire. Second sentence:
She is a man that has a job, no job, a car, no car,
To drive, driving. Tender is the money
That makes the bus *to go* over the bridge.
Go over the bridge. *Tender*
Are the postures singular verbally undressed men and women
Assume. *Strong* are the rivets of the bridge. "I'm not interested,
Try someone else." First sentence:
Wipe them off the face. Not complete.

Bold are the initiatives that break deadlocks
In the political arena of sexual nation states.
A bright flash I, the construct, embrace all my life
All the furniture in Furniture World, U.S.A. "first thing in the
     morning."
My head is somewhere in my head. *Say, threaten,*
Volunteer, want, all take the infinitive.
First sentence: *The woman's clothes volunteered*
To mean the woman's body. Biology
Is hardly the word. No irony, no misleading
Emphasis, just a smooth, hard, glossy desktop.
The President was "on the ceiling"
Where he could watch himself face down the faceless forces of history.

A nation's god is only as good as its erect arsenal.
It's so without voice, in front of the face, all my life I,
In corners, dust, accumulating rage breaking
Objects of discourse. "Why use words?" Smells from
The surrounding matter, the whole tamale.
"I have no idea" "I use my whole body"
"Be vulnerable" First sentence: *They were watching*
The planes to fly over their insurgent hills.
Second sentence: *Their standard of living*
We say to rise. No third sentence.

A HISTORY LESSON

I wonder whether "States" in "United States"
Is a noun or a verb. The clothes of my
Charmed wife I see before me, as the phone
Rings and rings. In the beginning, to set
The record straight, was a mother cooing to a baby.

US: What a wonderful audience
To put up with all dead people.
Push all the *right* buttons so we *won't*
Get blown up? Give the person back to the baby.

The higher the ladder one mounts . . . canceled.
We receive many helpful suggestions
Every day . . . The best of luck.

On high, money assumes a human look,
Like a face, that fine line
Between want and need.

"I use my whole doctrinaire
Vocabulary, praxis twice as hard
And rhetorical as a shotgun in a pickup.
Today's date, sigh, a heavily feathered
Paperweight crammed down the group esophagus
For pleasure. Your bored longings —

That's how money is manufactured."

A coy little cog beneath the Democratic Party
(Save the last dance for me) was born,
And now, suspended in a jar of methadone . . .

The United States unite into a fist standing tall,
Nothing to do all day but make war, this is not
My idea of a place to live. I'm willing to look
The text in the face, but am unable
Not to stay all the way outside, speaking
In infuriated detail. I'm a decal, you're a decal, unless . . .
Walter Mondale? Sappho? Separate
The living from the dead, right?
"If you say so, dead man."

PROBLEMS OF EVERYDAY LIFE

. . . canceled. I eat my words
And fall asleep. Sometimes there's a period,
Sometimes dots to connect, and sometimes
A blank. Bikini briefs and atoll.
Sometimes big flashes, big puns on light,
On flesh. Cherubs spill out

Of 2-D theory. We are fini, Lola,
Kaput, my vegetable scrub brush.
Take a very large number and be seated.
Boneless breast of plot, clock
As male archetype dozes, blazes through,
Pillar of living fire. ♫♫ All is calm, all is bright.

Dishes washed and dripping in the drying rack.
"So long as it is *there,* it holds the heavenly love"
That's what it says, "Aphrodite of the heavens";
Here, turned harlot, used words, Aphrodite of University Avenue.
Half a face, call 651-2524, tours, chariots.
Now I have to wash my hands.

PICTURE

Picture (see, control, dominate) a
Phallocentric lawyer dominating a Snickers, Milky Way, or Mars Bar
On Market Street in the spermy light
Of day. "I couldn't care less"

I'm not going to get off his case
Until the subject, a 10 foot tall ogre
Sulking at the conference table, changes nature.
Unknowable, domineering, ravening, question-begging, life-
Destroying, tune-mongering calliope. Always
At a moment's notice, water's edge, eye
Hems its own parade, sinks into the past. You can't believe
What you read. "I wouldn't if I were you"

For only in this way can the poem
Be returned to the mind (a mouth).
A man's large, erect penis and a woman's
Larger, more erect penis, these are the strategic materials

For the in-touch scenarios of people
Who husband the earth's increasingly scarce
Strategic materials. The mighty engine
Mounts the throne, of egg and semen made.

DON'T DRINK THE WATER, EAT THE FOOD, OR BREATHE THE AIR

My perfect life is being spoiled
By this shitty army food. Radioactive
Waters in the salad dressing are discoloring
My perfect pornographic page (the real thing),

Its thighs geometric, meretricious.
Torn-up grandmothers in El Salvador
My beautiful sky don't touch me or it'll go partly cloudy.
Envelope-language means nothing. Tear it open.

A number of other lives. Tears, cheers, applications.
So now you have a perfect one-inch vegetable word generator in my
    head.
It thinks. Stupid baby grown up extremely accurate.
Lob the applause meter right into the men's room at the Kremlin.

It is perfectly reasonable to be so annoyed
At the lack of respect one receives from the media
(Institutional acronyms spread putative paper legs
To a trillion dollar wind) that one thinks

Of the five hundred thousand dead communists
In Indonesia as sick caribou
Culled from the herd by the skilled PBS wolves.
This thin tundra snow makes a perfect backdrop.

MENTAL IMAGERY

My grandmother grew up on a farm
Somewhere in my mind. Estonia, I think.
There were no people there, only me.
Where once were vaginas like Bibles
And penises like bookmarks, now groups

Of chemically hounded hunters and gatherers
Huddle around the TV, a combination
Digestative and glory hole, glowing
In a permanent rightwing fundraiser
(The structuralist stunned in the tub,
The tide of signifiers [resumés] rising).

Now there is nothing wrong with having
A baby, though a few strategic needs might place
Childcare on the back burner. Somebody
Wants nobody in particular's oil. I want everybody
To talk. Tumultuous applause. I want everybody
(Letters literally burned into wood) to be home.
Unclean thoughts attach to counted bodies.

Here I am, man's clothes on a woman's baby.
The brain is a reducing valve, one
That doesn't work, watch. This salt shaker
(My features, irreducible)
Won't leave here without me.

UP MEMORY LANE

Give yourself one point for each time sense data mount
Up and suck you through the window. These
Single things left over from dream ovens.
Water makes a pretty picture.

date 2nd the on woman the of image sleep the said you love I
water aren't people. pore every from love Radiating

Why am I doing this?
Asks Dobie Gillis performing (imagine André Previn
Conducting Brahms on TV) cunnilingus on Annette Funicello
(You'll hear from my phallocentric lawyer).

Because you want to,
Need to literally like your own other.

life of facts the smear Words
desired you If. air real Through
weighed body your if, equally word Each
matter wouldn't direction then thought your as much As

But I've made my mind a land populated
way this in only for sound demons relations By
Can the poem enter the mind without
stopped effectively being and itself Disguising

SCAPEGOAT

Scraps of dogs in head, bacon. A big metal
Think tank cracks a smile, rolling down
Windows to shop the day away
To restore order. Walls call collect.
Spectators identify with the special effects

(Hear them barking?) as a beautiful industrialized
Woman, one in a million, rolls down her
Secret and drives over to your ad. My hands
(Welcome to the human race) are indefinably far
From my body. Rocky punches insurgent meat.
He'll lose. The withered plot thickens away.

Bitches of the World, unite, untie!
Male Presences, change your own diapers for a change!
Public buildings every ten blocks or so, solar, no doors!
A Poets Theater in every town!
Equip the stage with trampolines, but no P.A. systems,
No clocks, no extraterrestrial clues to meaning.

Back, earthling, to your partially eaten
Language tamer. Would you buy a used concept
From yourself? Then speak. A sentence (Here
We go again) whips itself into a frenzy of obvious
Obliterated social life. It's hazy & cool today.
The subject emerges from the rubble, ribbon,
Having survived, socially, partially eaten.

JOURNAL DES DEBATS

Another bumpersticker for peace. Another
Terrorist attack on the Word Bank. Terrorist
Is another word for entertainer. Entertaining
A numb mind is another bumpersticker for peace.

Alone on the court, a grandfather studies
His foul shot, and makes it.
Why should "impotent" mean
"Unable to maintain an erection"?

One doesn't own "the world," one owns
"Everybody else," plays a zero-sum game
Of squash, and stimulates one's partner
To orgasm (like learning to ride a bike)

With one's Weimar Republic sex manual,
Which led, without pause for thought,
To Nazi eugenics. People are now (still) alive.
He'll suck, if you can get him started.

PAPER

No progress

A dramatic monolog
At the moment of orgasm?

God of xerox,
God of blame,
Is your name
The same as mine?

Destruction from within
Begat sentence after sentence

Born to it

A fantasy blocks out
Colors in
The sun-noun

By the mental associations
Formed and bothered
Here, both in my
Mind and body and in
Conjunction with . . .

Presenting . . .

As told to . . .

Are you me?

It's so tangible it has
Talked day & night,
Hurts and offers
You a place
To stay for the rest of your life

Takes off shirt by river
Gets carried away
Gets put into warm delicious

Baked into nursery rhymes

Triangles, slaves

Not funny

No feeling, so very far away

In a cavern, in a canyon, excavating . . .

It was like learning
Another language only
To find that it's the same
One face way close now

Relates to objects
I'm afraid

You've got to
Drive em
And wash em
And show em that
You love em

Not a complete sentence
Afraid of the veils ripping
Afraid of the air burning

Isn't it funny,
There is a Pacific Ocean,
But no self?

Sounds like . . .

A picture of a head
Stares and would
Speak but there are words
Printed below on the paper
A common commodity
And naturally
You understand . . .

WHY USE WORDS?

A boatload of coruscating grunts
Arrives on Mars. Coruscating—
Think of a waterfall. Think of
An island paradise in the bank
Of the brain, think of jeeps, sand,

Native women, capitalized flesh, think
Of history as a communicated disease.
The deathbed scene in *Camille*.
Cleared to land. Slash and burn.
Think of photographed water,

Freely falling over a protruding lip,
Sparkling against a background of dead
Dirt and rocks slaving over the scenery.
"You take the boy delivering the tortillas,
Lock him in a room and beat the shit out of him.

Then you've two more names. Of course I'm just
Imagining it." I speak my whole life
Spread out against me in a collection
Of manipulable objects, all with realistic
Colors, prices, and accurate names.

"I'm in love, I'm in love
With a beautiful gal . . ." The image here
Is of a man eating chipped beef
On toast. Lines (greying red) appear
In the clotting medium . . . We study these.

Those mental patients on Grenada
Were so paranoid we had to
Kill them accidentally. Now we turn to study
The gods. Remember Mars and Venus caught
In that net? My doily is glowing a vicious red.

To sum up: Jack has got to find
The robbers' gold with the help of the dispossessed
Animals before he can go back home
And help with the chores (blindly chopping wood)
He used to find so hard and harder to understand.

EXCESS

Sometime around midlife, wishes
Gather to a locus (place)
(Take off your clothes and *place*
Them on the floor)

"Be vulnerable" skin softly
Switching tense (anything but that)
Go back to gather to a locus
(Remember who you are) (but who

Is that white vegematic on the counter
Of the redone dream lover's
Former mansion of a life?) Go back
To gather to a locus (memory: place)

(*Place* your mind in the refugee camp)
Go back to wishes gather
To a locus and begin to deny themselves
Nothing, not the slightest

Particle of certainty, vanity, face,
A vast (18" wide) and towering (72" high)
Perception (12" deep) of what is (there),
An ocean (mind) enraged, distended,

Swollen upright darker and colder green
Than tantrums or language. "I don't
Know you" Every rock on this tired
Uterocentric earth of language

In place, wrong, and to be
Read into the directions
By continuous
Approximate units of time.

STATEMENT

The universe is pronouncing sentences,
Nostalgic, what tense, and what
Person? I was about
To say, wholly in mind and body . . .
"You've had enough, buddy"

The Pentagon inhales its mystery religion
Of hydrogen bomb, outer regions'
Penetralia in recompense for attacks
On theory or shy good looks, orchestrated
To an overall bland finale

To logic-stories. If you lock yourself
Out of your car and you
Have left the motor running
And the car is in gear, moving
Away from you (this is not a test)

Then you are still not
Without transportation.
The dreaming senses (wake up and smell the burning rubber)
Reflect upon the sounds in the word
Water, by image or death or reason.

No place exists even once. Even before
Birth, earlier made-up syntax
Could tell you apart
From a thing or two, nothing waiting
In the wind, spiritual placebo plus

The actual problem of dying.
Common sense to speak after
Learning the language, but now
Come the interesting actual horrible
Mass concatenations. Think for awhile,

Not as a delaying tactic, and
Don't implode. So, the sun comes up,
Agreed? Not as some thermonuclear
Game of chicken, not the word, not
The movie. Hot water, chicken soup.

Unworldly broken credit card, one hand,
Two hands, three, four, five.
The Marshall Plan and our subsequent
Arms build-up was aimed at keeping Europe
From going neutral. A body,

Off the page, going native (how many orgasms can a paper tiger
    have?).
An occasional postcard, local news, but
National Geographic is not anybody's business.
Can you imagine having
Your body all its life,

Conscious, as a kind of record player
Of group life lived in the same
Place with other people you found
So fascinating that you learned to speak
Exactly the same language, plus personal

Surmises, sunrises interpenetrating
Dreams with real-time gargantuan
Optical dimension of the trees
Outside? In Guatemala in 1954,
Arbenz began to expropriate unused land,

Offering United Fruit exactly the same
Low figure United Fruit had given
Earlier as a basis to calculate taxes.
At that point, the CIA intervened.
There is a line, and it makes a picture,

A death's head revolving under strobed
News reports told to the excess orgasm
Skimmed off the xeroxed jobmobile
With distribution clear to all
Campus bookstores closed weekends

In a blinding drizzle of tears, one
Each day for life. "You won't
Be needing that" No effort
Of attention is ever wasted, vistas
Of sand, the one second it takes to memorize oneself on into story,

Pacified body asleep. No agreement
Without understanding the words are
Lawfully wedded illegal aliens
Tried by a jury of dazed responses
Splayed onto aging freeways, armed

With feelings that would choke a horse,
A thing with a tail, hanging down,
Relative to the greater mass of the earth.
The universe has spoken in here
Until it is many mornings ago

That I say this now here,
Orange there, told apart by the transoms
In memory wash breaking over
Body, water, different durations.
A crushed mind retains

Color, colors mingled in mindless
Alliances. The only thing standing
Between the Beverly Hillbillies and annihilation
Is not now and has never been
30,000 nuclear bombs.

INSTITUTIONS & THE INDIVIDUAL APPLICATION

Is this my ballot? This
Plastic placemat (don't stop, don't stop)
Showing a man and a woman
In a refugee camp listening to a loudspeaker?

Eleven million children (picture it)
(Don't stop) standing on the surface of the earth
(Scarface) looking at a lightbulb.
The plot? I don't know you.

Second mortgages, pallbearers
On a roll, seeded lawns,
It's lights out at the fetish factory.
Think of these modified nouns (this luminous egg

Is your body), selected and torn to pieces
Of these modified nouns, as the
Orgasmic (that word again) drumroll
(Look out the window) (his phallocentric

Truth goes marching on) leading to
A giant phallus (male walrus)
Sworn to uphold language (your museum or mine?).
Day: cars; night: trees,

No original word, many
Per body, father and baby
Cooing back and forth, mother
And son talking.

CLIFF NOTES

Because the languages are enclosed and heated
each one private a separate way
of undressing in front of the word window
faces squashing up against it
city trees and personal rituals of sanitation
washing the body free of any monetary transaction.

The parts of the machine take off their words and die away
in a description read to the senses
by the leftovers on TV that no one would think of eating
even in the very act of swallowing.

It's these "very acts" that we must
Pay attention to the flatness of the screen now!
For it's this very flatness
that the fraily projected containment of the humanized body
is designed to be pinned to
by, naturally, forces outside our control.

It can't be the knobs' fault because this is back before knobs.
Rock ledges, laurel fumes, sacred fainting spells
later on in the very pictures written, this is back before the alphabet
the pictures of the rocks in the savant's eye
he's chained to these pictures by the sententious wriggle
of the buttocks two classes down, whose owner
can hardly speak, can't multiply, and stands there waiting for Plato
to have Socrates tell him he's only rhetoric.

But, as we know from Aristotle, Plato doesn't know any plots
he can only give orders, dipping himself diffidently into the material
    signifier at the same time as the ripples he thinks he's thinking into
    their roundness come back to haunt him in the form of crude jokes
    about his square calves at unprestigious dinners. In fact, he looks a
    little like that table he's always using as an example.
Next come the Romans, and with them we first see the sky
artificial creation of scarcity of meaning
spread out over the proletariat as a visible economic ether.
You can look, but it costs.

We can still see traces
of the tracts where they lived
and can still understand their language
which consisted entirely of dirty jokes about money.
It's easy to clear away the froth of biology
with a few commands
to reveal the naked postcard of ageless windwashed marble
posing for recorded history.

SPEECHES TO A CITY NO LARGER THAN THE REACH OF A SINGLE VOICE

One says: My method involves
causing my impervious bucket
in a very real way, to enter a particular wave
in a particular place, so that the aperture
admits exactly enough water to fill the interior
bucket as sentence, with the handle, handle as readership
chained to the benches of the galley
by my earlier terminological conquests
of the formerly merely wet ocean
now charted, drawn & quartered, so that
my trireme is as if self-propelled
and is, in a very real way, unsinkable.

The other says: I have no method.
I merely undress in powerful moonlight
delighting the wretched few
and plunge in and drown each time.

I say: I turn to *Dallas*, to baseball, to Prince, sushi, fractals
—note the intrusive plane of explanation
tied up finally in some diplomatic pouch of noncombatant pro-life
    pro-choice pre-ontology movie-like stasis—I mean
a person, in quotes, on earth, quotes
sited in the aporia of toilet paper in Nicaragua
of jobs in Youngstown, if you don't already own the shopping center
    then go shopping, which is why in the later afternoon on weekdays,
    after the heat of the searing sexual repression and age war of
    midday has abated, and the talk shows have grown cool and
    delightfully empty with discussions of kitchens and embarrassing
    moments
which allows the viewer to go out and turn
theory into practice, in short
to rule the world
until the news at six enacts the State . . .

And now I see that some enchanter has spoken my words.

WE

We have come here today to be plural
sit in rows or sprawl
in the wind-tunnel of design competition
to find out how many a dollar will buy
eyes focused on the spinning disk, the picture.

Everyone is singular
impersonating corn gods, matching colors
mating, prying apart the lifestyle
of the class above
detached priests, angels with wings of erotic syntax.

Have we agreed on the plot?
Apparently not.
The stories get squashed: colorless incomprehensible bits dehydrating
    on Consumer's tray
or they grow larger than life:
day after day of Reagan's sense of humor.

We get left off in Afghanistan
that solemn trysting place of the advanced ascetic journalist.
A woman, of indefinite age, dressed as Truth, is seen (note
the passive), veiled
coming down a long winding dusty path
so slowly that, some centuries, she seems
not to advance at all (please turn to page 37)

UNVEILING THE VEIL

People, by the sheer weight of their words
going faster & faster
so many cars
following the law of large numbers
on pale cement
all in someone's army
if not Freud's then
God's, to alleviate the guise
of separated life histories hanging like coconuts against the tragic
    generic background of the sky-father, ocean mother sans article
    overwhelmingly near lapping at the small shells on the beach ranked
    by intensity of experience
kept going with no apparent break
toward the same circle of emoluments
plus a lot of oil to keep the working parts apart
i.e., you & me.

If not these words then others.
Which false consciousness I wind in the face
of the scattered myth of speech
that lights the nightly disguise of city plans
money growing enemies under the buildings
faster than the stuck semiosis of their glamorous little portals
can stretch a would-be sentence
from mirror to broken mirror.
Originally the clothes were full of holes but they ended up invisible.

Some words which can't be others.
A well-formed system, with disappearances.
News on the hour from a cloud or cloud-like building
to be precise: nowhere
doubled over, a circle
whose circumference is refugee camps and whose meaning
trapped in the no-nonsense enunciation
"You have not yet been sentenced to death" I'm
in the center of that, 1700 mile per hour winds
"not yet" radiating outward.

STREETS

There's no history in the past.
Nothing happens there anymore.
A brown twilit civic peace
oozes mesolithically from the clumps of ancient houses.
The narrow alleyways are collagenous
a mat of dusty humus nourishing
the squat human stalks. Fake sky gods
take care of the plot.
By the end, Pinocchio is a real boy.

At its première, history was received poorly.
Catharsis was a slap in the face
as the spectators watched themselves
being measured, killed, inflamed, conscripted, armed to the teeth,
    inventoried, invented, in a word
loaded onto the train.

the face, race, fate—words blurred
in the upset crowd noise—
something, at any rate, was suddenly precious
torn, out of reach, available
at a price, too high to pay.

For the general populace, it was discrete
leftover images: newspapers stacked on the back porch, the smell of
    the Chinese restaurant spreading across the tracks and the reddish-
    green sumac
episodic, meaning less & less after each commercial.

It is on these unmaintained tracks
that the stories, Ann Landers, *Dynasty*, the shapes of the cars
arrive in the form of a thoughtless city
run by minds whose characters (the letters of the name)
are complete, not to be altered
certainly not by what happens.

The towers are visible from far away.
The land beneath is valued at the inhabitants' food shelter &
    transmission of

lacunae the soft shredded pages go here
between the rows of traffic.

ANTI-OEDIPUS

The city is dying because you killed your father, could have been
    anyone
and are sleeping with your mother? No
problem. Cut out the eyes that deny one and one
is one. *"Get back in the house!"*

Inside the house (note the word
standing solid, timbered, painted, mortgaged, but that's okay
because the calendar, white alabaster that it wants to be
works in silent invisible ways
on committees too numerous and boring to name, they never make
    the papers
Celtics win at buzzer
to build my tomb in advance.

So many buildings and leins jutting their private languages
into one another's views, New York could be
the unconscious, or, equally, heroically
consciousness itself, and no one would be any the wiser
because, while the details are being worked out
they're also smothering the crystalline
—don't blink, you'll spoil—combatants, combinations
the lock no one would pick for parents
and the stage seems to be moving
the actors are falling apart
the trees are losing their leaves.

If only the plot would leave people alone
like a tie in a box on a shelf in a store
to absorb the intensities of their decoration.
What I need is a single body.

WORD STIMULI

I am split, it is written
parallel lines pressing powerfully together.
Past & present (which came first?)
—one growing more obvious all the time—
went down to the mouth, one fell in and

Facts as shrines, with the isolated object theory
just doing its job
alongside the soft buttery throes of word stimuli
like "war" makes Nietzsche excited
and "pity" pitiless.

The Bible, drawn & quartered, says what it says
in the silence of a public execution.
To get near the forbidden
description of the body, read
the victim's mother's face in the paper
examine the murderer's corpse
and note the fall of clods in the field blown up by dynamite
simply to be able to get the seeds in the ground.

Inside this split, the body
with its secret names lies open
like a fresh dug grave to the Almighty
fathered by no one, thunder billowing through
the rent scenery to overpower speech.

In the cave a quick intense mating between sound & meaning.
White shorts & jogging thighs emerge pulsing as one
the Third World safely tucked away
inside some disadvantaged individual's search for a meaningful form
in which to write
down his or her experience
or just hope the letter gets printed
in USA TODAY
cheap distribution good sports four colors and rapidly becoming
    dematerialized
because, because *nothing*.

COMMUNICATION

Personal experien-
ces, one, maybe two
at a time. You, me . . . H—o—l—d it . . .
Photos, raisins, buds on boughs, nipples.
As anybody on earth has remarked.

Punctuation is all
what? Wet
slippery categories invite thought.
Milk it or eat it? you? that?
This is why we have minds

or, at least,
"I hear you."
Off the record
is jungle, and Tintin grows up to be Claude Levi-Strauss.
There's a whole thought back there, a series, a seminar, a sacred city
    rotting in the reruns, ruled by Hollywood gods or dinosaurs,
    bisected along external blame lines by Vegematic ads at 2 A.M. . . .

A mind shines
in the glare of its partialities
stares at views, monsters
hiding under boulders backed up on the image screen
matter married to tourguide, Sassooned doghair on vacuum needle, if
    only you see exactly what I

Personal, plural, inside the meat, no middle terms, eternal,
    exterminism, fried life, the ratings war with Russia, the Gap, over
    here, me, the one in the mind, orgasm right on the vinyl, live,
    almost, the machine with a brain, the slogan that uses words.
Rocks, submerged
set spoon to river in a jumprope rhyme
laundry hanging out back, Jack
so your mother's still around you, literally, with commas for sense
    organs, meal-like adjectives, lack of self and worship the serfs,
    literary examples toiling in the over-sexed landscape.

And thus description is artificial
insemination of the intellect
by an inflamed romance
of the universality of knowledge.
"Put it down anywhere."

The city on a hill
ruled, quadratically
by Hitler slash Duchamp slash the future.
People are now alive, large numbers
waiting to go in a thermonuclear exchange, the Big Potlatch.

A land has been laid down, back & forth, like it said it says, always
    already changed, spoken friability of monumental air set in stone
    between first coos and the final cessation of sense in heart-felt
    clichés, expandable, finite, the breeding of phrases in breaths
across which the actual
caress of seconds
or what pass
for units of attention

in the only sequence imaginable
(after the fact)
punctuated by tantrums (see the past
(Mommy & Daddy (God is dead but all the more God)
periodically destroyed

but on the near side of noun-like nation-states
grading the flanks of the spoken body
cutting off circulation and bombing off the record, not with words
whoever's not smiling & waving at the hot, tired, pictured soldiers,
    who have been flown thousands of miles to receive the thrown
    flowers the express wishes of the dead.

UNTITLABLE

The little man inside the last individual brain
To approach the heart of darkness on the front page
I have to dress this manikin here
and squirt adrenalin over its visual field
driving apart first come first serve dreams
a blue car backing up, an aggressive lunch
pieces of the person puzzle itself
the one with the face in the front, sympathetic responses
hanging down fleshy, attractive
a voice in the wilderness crying
Build me a city and buy me a drink, take all my time and make me a
    street
down which no robbed crowd of punks . . .

Who told me these things about no one
ways off the track, as if the reader (touché)
were a living body
(touché) built of chance, needs
and a systematic refusal to look at the military details
an obviousness that the lobbies seminars luxury boxes
all the forms of having one's cake and eating it then & there
in the face of the ontologic mystery that has created
so few jobs
and the spaces of entertainment so vast

Now that the Super Bowl is over
and God has come back to life
in the form of a man in a suit of TV
machined to a fineness that a woman rained on in a bender at
    Greenham Common
breaking into clauses: that I own the land *which* you do not *because*
    you haven't broken & entered the library *where* time gets turned
    into money *that* grows on trees *which* tradition says are
    sticks impregnated *by* the systematic force *of* the earth's rotation . . .
Emphases grow thick as history snowballs.
Waves of rage police the objects.

GROWING UP

The little devil is happy swinging on the gates of Hell
and I have only to hear myself say "Sit down and *eat your dinner!*"
to hear the hinges creak
oiled with the human integer
raised to the highest power.

Next to the gate, a stream is running
always a little further on and
there's always water to drink and a dry throat
because the hellish mistake the historicized body
the dividing mind the newspaper hat the sunnysideup president
Stand back! Get some water somebody! He's fainted or faking or
   painting a picture of such insuperable force . . .

And you thought battleships meant jobs.
And thought meant you or books and rebellious
romance after hours, beer on the stereo
all the illegible ills capitalism spells
on schizophrenia's know-nothing body.

Like "bulwark" in sci-fi spaceships
there is "process" and "structure"
and "an obscure desire to run one's finger
round the rim of the cup in time
to the eternal return of Bastille Day."

And there is, and here
the list came on like puberty, silent and internally enormous
fallen from some great height
and the devil felt a roar of benevolence rushing through the veins of
   his forehead as his instincts mated, each with a word, like a mass
   Moonie wedding, only the God of State had fallen apart, and the
   cisterns, pipes, aqueducts, barns, cribs were full, and earth was
   matter, running water, people, asleep possibly, or amused by their
   non-narrative bodies.
It was like talking, the whole language at once, it *was* talking, me
   talking, say anything and I scatter.
Helicopter shadow rides up the side of the apartment house.

LET'S SAY

A page is being beaten
back across the face of "things."

Inside me there's a little book of no color, its pages riffling as I
    breathe, a moving point, torn out

and I read this scrapbook of desire
let's not say constantly
asleep & provoked by the economics of cliffs, galleys, cartoons,
    explosive devices patterned to look like adults reading signs
casually, very fast

and in this wind, leavened by sun
or am I merely reading that
backwards, inside the restaurant where they serve the parts
by number, innuendo
and the you and the I spends its life
trying to read the bill
alone in the dark
big wide street lined with language glue

A page is being written.
It's fun to chew, to work things out
to close the damn book
to sit in the sand with a radio
no bikini no tan line no body
a dream matchup
you can either be in or out, no middle ground
the floor is sexualized, tessellated with little languages crying out speak
    me, squash me, love me up into one libidinous hunk of noise, you
    great big missing other, yoo-hoo, over here

and the finished word is an album of past pleasure

smoking out one last incomprehensible nuance beside still waters
that talk their talk

of which you are the noun
the one & only

and the model breaks, leaving
a nasty little landscape which *you*
and the group of course
the other the slaughtered city the strafed farms
silently
in large heated buildings
the smell means money
and the classics are being straddled
a page is being beaten
O parse me, says the son to the so-called absent father
in a windbreaker by the lakefront in Cleveland
sixty degrees and a fishing pole
the breeze or am I reading water again

THINGS

Reification won't get you out of the parking lot.
Nor will mastery of the definition of sounds
in the throat, the bottomless pit, out of which
these things which we, transparent, self-refuting
hold to be self-evident.

Glamor of the thing, childcare
of the name, where language
is a diorama, with the mortal speaker
licking the glass to taste
the quasi-divine intervention of answerable syntax

holding out an empty glass
for water, *New Yorker* poetry-water
New York Times rational apolitical germ-free water.
(Take it off, take any one little piece of it
all off.)

As Gertrude Stein writes
in language—the Riviera
of consciousness—"Thank you
very much," though what service
we the reader have rendered . . .

And who is this "they"
who have terrorized all sentient let's not say "beings"
with the plurality of their buildings
the notions in their texts set up
to test you & me (proud little ones & twos)?

Who are they who so greyly
evade address, preferring instead
to throng the stadiums and airwaves
and glacial showrooms with their incessant
economic comeon/putdowns of the you/I person/psychopath
    state-squashed figurines
with our looks that could kill and in fact
do kill but never them.

Thence come the crooked smokes
of our psychodramas, which they relish
like the notes of the *Goldberg Variations*
whole histories pounded into simple binaries for lunch
Bovary/non-Bovary, with no calories because no body
you've got that one, and I've got *this* one
and the city doesn't fit in the eye.

So one, sad triste morte
goes all the way home to zero
with its blinding simile reflecting the furniture
off the original digit standing there
back in the frozen reified narrative of the parking lot
a past you can count on
safest investment
without things to get in the way
of the simple law of outward push.

THE ART MACHINE

The art machine hits the beach running hard.
But the beach, let's take a break and think
about the fact of the beach. Metal treads
vs. linguistic mucus, oceanic repetition vs.
one-time bodies, let's really get a two-step going here
structuralism dressing the baby in pink or blue.

Pay tribute to the tribal noon.
Somebody has to. There's a body everywhere you
The street corner, the right angle
the proverbial son of a bitch
scanning the territory from his post-verbal helicopter.

The tertiary form of the blades going round.
It's not castration, not capital flight, just noise.
No adequate substitute for childhood
on the ground in easy range, unwilling to die
Cut

Petting the dog and being polite
asking about the dog, birthdays
clodlike remnants of the big mouthfilling hours
following instructions from the dear dead past, housebroken, inside
where one flatters the grains to count them so thoroughly
as they fall through the aperture.

The army needs parts and the parts need
a job to do. The sentences are based on
complete lives, not thoughts. The principle of equivalence
takes your breath away to feed the engine
because without the engine being on
the tank can't move and make its point.

And the great chain of being
suspended over the educational buildings
lashing down, forming an up out of fragments of knowledge
"polished" floors vs. "cheap" cinderblocks
This broken figure of knowledge, personified and funded
head reaching heaven, stalks out to revenge its brutalized shape
there in the shine of each fender, this loathing
for the fact of the strange neighbor's glance invading
one's individual odor and the right to a fair trial
in the privacy of one's unremembered dreams.

Various bugle blasts at dawn, or what passes away
with no resale value, time a single line of words
terminable or interminable, it takes a golden android
whose sex is colored lights to find out
and the who who cares is condemned
to biological immediacy and release
the excited puppy's tail knocking its water over.

FABLE

A story without an end is like a person
who's still alive, metonymous with Cleveland
which means that he can die for Cleveland's right to exist
in Central America perhaps, or wherever
Cleveland might care (personification) to project its existence.

More like on Sixth Street, bottle in bag in hand
a metaphor for his situation's grasp of him
clever structure the city but just a few too many executives
tangled in the spidery caress of the car ghost
who leaves an order for 40,000 windshields at midnight
and the hero wakes up damaged next morning
having slept with a rusty door.

From Cleveland, one gets invited on many voyages
mainly to countries where the government
has the scenery half under control. Even a dog
can tell the background apart
from its bulging brown & white tummy.

For the people, we have a private novel to walk around in
singular, forbidden, lusty, a page turner, mirror cover
all smothered over in a creamy layer of jealous syntax
equaling the desire to know where your children are
at all times, or, if a child yourself, where you are, for all time.

So a map
nothing fancy
just the piece of paper the teacher
puts on the wall.
All prior wars have been concluded.

Cuts heal, though children
read their skin
as a too-vivid fairy tale where, beneath the happy ending, the monster
    lives
bright red, ready to surface at the slightest conflict
to force a conclusion.

THE BROKEN MIRROR

From the stately violence of the State
a classic war, World War Two, punctuated by Hiroshima
all the action classically taking place on one day
visible to one group in invisible terms
beside a fountain of imagefree water
"trees" with brown "trunks" and "leafy" green crowns
50s chipmunks sitting beneath, buck teeth representing
mental tranquillity, they sit in rows
and read their book and the fountain gushes forth
all the letters at once, permanently
a playful excrescence, an erotic war against nature.

And here's a check for five feet of shelf
in the life-after-death book club, seminar upon seminar
grains of sand the tan body rests on
glorious huge & hypothetical
worth all the bad press human sacrifice has received.

Outside, masses of angry numb matter blow against the symphonic
    angles of the citadel, warm & witty with electronically modulated
    voice, the earnest look out of the sweater, microphone hidden
    casually in memory, clouds a diversified portfolio of sensation.
The pictured body is relaxed & smooth
on the unmade bed, maple syrup, the waffle drenched
not a sentence, a way of life, the way out.

But I don't want to have to recreate the very ground of being
it's supposed to create me, like it said it did already
intelligibility aside, monumentality of social decay aside,
food & water & explanations of hierarchies to last a lifetime
aside, out of the way, out to a lunch of human bit parts broken under
    the State.
I don't want to improvise, in a foreign language
my own, but in the wrong mouth, my own
a parody of my mostly silent dreams, I don't want to
—I'm melting, all my lovely inwardness—make love
to the middle of the World Bank's picture of the person.

Let language, that sports page of being
mystify its appearance in all speech writing thought tonight
so that the thing, that object of burnished flirtation
can smuggle out the self, that drill bit . . .

But why am I contracting for the construction of this life-like
    place-like spilling-over lived-in
if only for a moment or memory-shape, since readwriting is a mirror
backwards at best, of prior intent
while you sit before me (note the you-as-I circuit, banquet with masses
    of flowers, choirs, cranial blooms lit up, sacred, edible

BINARY

Two heads are better than one.
Sunlight on the grass is better
than the power to dissolve oneself
into a variety of blades.
The declarative sentence
cut
lash die kill interrogate clear away
the blood-soaked body
no longer here the declarative sentence
would be something other than what it
says except that "you are what I am"
is to "the unspoken forces that surround us"
as "sunlight," see above, is to
"mental furniture," trashed, sat on
in state, loved, its wheels licked far into the night
sirens, thighs, the whole gizmo going off
or not
and then why bother, except
already bothered on both sides

Finally the I writing
and the you reading (breath still misting the glass)
examples of the body partitioned by the word.
Pie in the sky, tons, suspended
over one's heads
by a single declaration of desire.

A tragic curse
is dripping down generations
making mincemeat of the fully grown and operational
person, whose mother
may have said goodnight in the violet light
projected down the individual hall
in such a way that novel
was complete
inside that gesture.

All it needed were other people
in sufficient quantity
and limited lifespans.

In realtime drama, however, people suck
and what eventually lets down
is some earlier story
they only find out about later
chopped to bits somewhere barely on the map.
The spectators, duly echoing
in the amphitheater, must find
what identities they can.

WORD WORLD

Gentle analogists rock the surface
of the inhabitable word. *I*
am the earth, the sun, the moon
the taste of bread, the place

of sex and death. That's why
there are tears at weddings, jokes
at funerals, and animated projections at birth.
Doesn't logic depend on tact?

And if reality has toes to be stepped on
I have whole Patagonias of emotional red ink
taught to the rule of a spiritualized
virtu-laden hickory stick, strict, unspeakable
bodies dying to pronounce its name.

PERSON

Eats, drinks, sticks pipe in mouth and asks
What society (books on varnished desk, vanished races, where have I
    smelled that smell before I was born, a kind of hard-headed
    pragmatism standing in the empty spaces . . .
What society has ever failed to fashion a human
receptacle for its narrative wastes?
C'est la guerre the garage the riding mower
the obtrusive stories that don't stop when the sun goes down physically
low blood sugar lowering the vocabulary utilization
the world universe mind of god cushioning the fall of the dead letter
water coming into the river from an unknown source.
Sometimes you just have to go lie down with the unnamed by-products.

They have no names, not because people are stupid
but because there's no place on the tray to put all the slides.
Plus the fact that food is fashion and thus
bites the hand that eats it
or, to put it differently
the Great Salt Flats are the thighs of what conceivable being
the wood from whose Proust no contractor
no matter how liberal the building code
glass houses conceived in sin from day one
blizzards of chance down upon the fountain of youth
all without a verb
because capitalism makes nouns
and burns the connections.

Words get forced, like the fugitive in *The 39 Steps*
into making a speech about what? ending in cheers with the speaker in
    handcuffs.
And in fact one's own crudely physical body has never been in this
    second before, it's less likely than it looks, imagine a TV growing
    legs and talking, if a TV could talk we wouldn't understand it.

The intimate journal protects its secrets.
The intimate flesh projects its secrets.
In the bathroom: Kill a (Jew crossed out) Nazi.

OEDIPUS REX

Extinct cites, their driven people still visible
in old sounds, I'll have to make this brief, time
to go, birds flying south, I'm double parked, here
comes Kreon now, just as we are mentioning him.
What news, ancient uncle, from the transcendental desktop?

KREON: The people, hemmed in by liberal playgrounds
and rightwing communication systems, are dead
or dying. No one's complaining, mind you, but with the inauguration
    just hours away the sky seems to be crumbling, and the decibel level
    in some stadiums is below that of Mallarmé's tomb.
God thought you should know.

OEDIPUS: Tell God that I've got a family and long hours
of being myself to consider, how to explain things
so that meals don't degenerate into chaos and we eat
each other, like your nation states.
It would be like nuclear winter to me if I couldn't support my family
    with the sheer flexible power of my separated words.

KRE: God wants you to die.

OED: Tell God that my desires are infinite, if unfit
for human consumption. Sense perception
is a thing of the past. Myths spill over
into the present. I'm one
with the machines that go boom in the night.
You may be a mere bureaucratic bug in the rug, a sad hole with an
    abstract smile coming home to roost on your obsessed statue
but I've got a problematic nest egg of involuntary memory, I
    remember most of my old girlfriends, personal stuff, priceless, but
    not so very interesting to you or God or anyone else. So finally
I'm just going to say no
to physical forces, matter, and predestination.

KRE: Since you're going to die, God wants to see you repent.

OED: You can reprint any of my old speeches
but I doubt God will be able to tell them apart from anything anyone
    else ever said.
I think I'll just stand pat.
I never meant to soliloquize, but since the government's gotten so big
    and secret, any jerk with an open mouth turns out to be in the
    center of an infinitely expanding universe of gloom and doom, each
    sound that comes out, even if it's just asking where there's a
    bathroom downtown, contains lonely world-shattering forces,
    Magellanic clouds, hot winds to obliterate all human obstruction.

But keeping silent just subsidizes television.
And the past is so addictive, it takes longer and longer . . .
It all turns into a story, like my body . . .

THE REAL LANGUAGE OF MEN

I am an artificial
event, a moral, made of parts, non-recurrent.
But if I had been told at birth that I was to have both
a body and a country, and that
one would have to be balanced on the other,
like the quantification of knowledge has to be balanced
on the representational, presidential head of a pin,
that meanwhile I would be breathing the monitored air
where the softly cubed contours of the schoolrooms shout, IN GOD WE
    TRUST,
capitalized, which you'd better not be too cynical about,
says the small print, when you go to buy a car or a can of beer—

Insofar as one day's name does follow another
and they do have numbers,
then time does form a linguistic base,
a place where sentences can and do occur.
But you, young person, will have to go away,
so say goodbye to the calendar pictures
the early years were pointing towards
and go and sit somewhere and don't come back until your body fits
    into the language.

If not, do I have to be an abstract infant again?
I can understand the cars
if I identify with the way they rhyme
lined up waiting for the light to change,
and I can only do that if I came to life
in a cubed playpen, a quantified controlled place
of uniform illumination, where every hour is born equal.

This light shines over the ads,
the dead language everyone reads by nature
but no one gets to speak.
It goes unsaid, unsayable, breaking apart
into two unusable chunks, country and body.

It pays to identify with money, the unit value of the scale,
not to watch the clock but to be the clock, to desire freedom
through quantification of desire. What kind of a world is it
where anything can only mean something else,
and where there is a choice of kind of world?

The citizen is to pry the concrete particulars loose, connect and
    animate them, freeing them for experience to experience, is that it?
A long-shot self-expressiveness which leads to lifelong self-criticism
    and serialization, movie rights dangling tantalizingly beyond the
    fingertips?
I think you eventually end up with some kind of certificate.
So, in conclusion, give me a society of smashed-in cubes, a place to
    stand, and a head of pre-owned words, and I will move the earth,
    write my name, do the dishes, and be myself.

BACK TO THE PRESENT

Not I, but the Gross National Product, the mushroom-like military
    sump pump whose flow charts spring up at midnight,
producing scenarios whose orders are written on water
which is then shredded, followed by machines and a lightly
    personalized number:
you work on identifying with it when you deposit checks.

Not these words, but the cars accelerating by,
not so much using the space
as training brains for the random input of want
in a ritual known as the history of the world,
the real language of men,
as I'm rolled through owned quadrants,
utterly out of office, a spectator
smashing away, after the fact,
into the represented pulp of this page.

The names of the countries can change, once a week, once a month,
the rate can change, the male newsperson looks concerned
but truly neutral, his mouth the epicenter
of objectivity, the great good place, saying simply
that the army is stepping in,
no figures on casualties are available
because there's not enough causality outside the studio to go around.
Turning to traffic on Route 80 it looks like
the spectre of abstraction has finally been made real.

While the committee of my words
argues down the page in California and utopia
at the same time—that was a joke—
the state governs by a shot of the H-bomb going off to each his own
followed by one of a guy coming between a pair of tits you can't argue
    taste.

That's totally false, uncommitted, melodramatic acting-out, fifty-year-
    old wedding cake hysteria which I resent having written to the
    depths of the clear air of my neutral reading-mind
vs., in fifty million heads, the picture of the time car taking off from
    the ground, back from the past, disappearing into the future,
    powered by lovable household garbage, and the music, go back and
    redo history and none of this will have happened, it's perfect this
    time, a perfect place to stop.

FLAT MOTION

There is a store, it is an individual,
like you, me, a body, corporate,
you or I might go into this store and see racks
of cardboard boxes covered
with a picture and with words on the back
whose typeface is neutrally available
while the title on the front reaches out
by some marked variation, something to call
my own as the song goes, above the picture
from the movie taped in theory
inside the boxes if they were full but these
are just display copies, before we pay
we can only look at the one picture.
But I've forgotten to ask your name.

In the movies there's usually half a cemetery
under the new houses, or a forceful intervention
down memory lane leads to a dynamic new present
in which there's sex and money for everybody
except the bully, who has to wax your box until it shines.
But a movie is a graveyard out of which each corporation
has about four months to get his or its money back
before it's dropped, like last year's hieroglyph for death,
onto the obscure back pages of the pyramid walls.

We're mad as hatters—naturally, working with all these chemicals—
and we're not going to take it anymore! We're not going to
make them any more! We're not going to pay for them any more!
Or take them home and polish them, we're not
going to exaggerate, mask, drive somewhere else
in a crisis-like stupor, where's the store, why isn't
one here? We're dissolving, as they fly above
the hellish stretches of weekly news magazine prose where irony
    presses us flat.
Hell is not other people, hell is the non-dimensional
back of a balance sheet, the place where other people,
i.e., *you*, live, put the kids on the bus, and see an occasional flat movie.

We don't want this, not to mime defeat again and again
in individual phrases, faces, lines that have so much flavor
your memory can be insured for millions,
the person metaphor can be picked up over and over
in a thousand songs, let's get out of here, they sing,
go for a walk, just you and me and the seven basic plots.
If this were a silent movie, the part where I get to make this speech
would be reduced to the clothes I happened to be wearing,
the background, the look of the room I was in,
and how I operated in the frame. Arms engaged, glance connected,
    face projecting,
the song stops and says, It's not the way
you own your hair, or the car you drive in limbo every day,
but the way you can, not quite leap tall buildings, or convert wide
    factories
with a single word, not that either, not that easy.

THE FREEZE

I remember my thighs.
It was in a movie. I was asleep,
but voting, trying to remain inconspicuous.
I saw what I saw and I felt what I felt.
At the time I thought nothing of it,
but as the policewomen started to remove her blue blouse it was my
    mother and I was Stendhal and the mercury was starting to wear off
    and I was sick, sick with desire the soundtrack suggested, but really
    just plain sick, damaged, an exception, the only one in the non-
    named bourgeois world who was separated from desire. I had no
    job except to be witty entering salons, profound later in the
    evening, and rhapsodically convinced of my doubt in private, when
    I would throw my wig in a corner and write of the dangers of
    satisfaction, running with the pack in the pre-dawn

A body is a whole thing.
A life is parts.
There's no way to verify these statements.
No one *has* a body. Skin, smell, or aura is the line
below the bottom line, where private property stops.

Do I get to say
what it means? Only
if Vietnam was an allegory.

The king is still in his counting house,
his index finger pointing at
the first gold piece, his mouth
pronouncing the number one.

Though we don't have a king any more.
We have a complex system of networks,
advertisers dangling from writers dangling from cameramen dangling
    from stockholders.
But then what's the subject under discussion?
now that we live in an ever-expanding political movie,
where an Uzi is a dick or a calculator,
cheaper every year, but it's confusing,
even for the lifestyles of the rich and famous,
to have bodyguards but, again, no body.
So the famous face freezes, contemplative, while the voice-over says, I
    remember my thighs, feet, the sidewalk, standing outside, red sky,
    watching ants, but the frame only stays frozen for the credits.

THE VIEW FROM THE DOLLAR BILL

The top of the pyramid sees everything
while the brick on the bottom sees nothing special out of the window:
an air shaft, a park, a well-kept car across the street, a woman ignoring
    a man denouncing a phone pole,
miles of sand. I am my life,
one says. The bricks, the words, phone poles, pyramids
voices in every layer say this.

As long as there's even one category
there's room for improvement, and nothing else, all the way to the
    top,
everybody has that right.
If one pyramid gets too crowded, start your own.

If you're a slave you want to run away,
but only to where there's no slavery.
The will isn't magical, overseers pounding those bricks
into nearly identical shape, the Wednesday Night lineup, the Thursday
    Night lineup.

All the episodes, contemplated one by one, become monuments
enclosing a dead divinity, a vivid picture of what it must be like
to actually exist. The monarch surveys his land
and under the potency of his view, the peasant women all get
    pregnant.
But if you hate your mother,
think how you'll feel staring at a video terminal all day.
Then there're these other places where you get to kill time, if nothing
    else.

On my father's TV, the host celebrates himself by taking whole towns
    in his mouth and mentioning them for up to ninety seconds.
At that rate, how long will it take to stand the existing art/money
    intersection on its point?
And what will that do to the way things look?

Each bill states, Pay to the bearer of this slab, one vivid picture,
and he will live on his father's television forever
or ninety seconds, whichever comes first.

SEX

Ed Meese is not relentless necessity.

History puts on its hanging cap
and looks for all the world like it's about to
pronounce sentence. The desire to rhyme, to master
rules, the ruler, the ruler's uncontrollable urges,
to be the one who speaks, who says anything,
how does the old song go? "The State is a person
who never shits or fucks
but manfully defends its property
from sexual attack by a display of pomp
that puts use to shame and shame to use."
All it needs is enough music.

Meanwhile is was midnight. The sentence groped hurriedly for some
    flimsy rhetoric, but things were too clear. The historical camera was
    rolling, the grammar grinding, moans and groans filled the
    soundtrack precisely, like food in airline trays, far away but in theory
    edible.

I too read the comics and see the gods
wolfing down lasagna. Now that the calendar is an endangered species,
    I directly perceive, by intuition,
single things, brown wrappers on magazines at all night stores,
see-through wrappers on the toilet paper, isolate commercial songs
to be picked up one at a time, crossed off the list,
paratactic, the shopping list like Homer, epic shopping,
but Odysseus never had to stand in line in his life.

So, yes, critique the three-gun ship of state
that shoots out a bright yellow Big Bird talking gently but stupidly
    about how hard it is to share,
critique the Contra snuff films they show in the diplomatic pouch
    dangled darkly before the White House regulars who dutifully
    shout out, "Take it off!"
to the counterrhythm of ♪♪ "I'm going to ed-it
my shop-ping list, down by the river side."

With this VCR I thee watch take off your clothes and make love into
a speech about democracy, when what I actually want
is democracy, and for the busses to be as well made as the bombs now
    are.

Sorry, but when I woke up this morning my aura
was all over the front page. The cropduster
nose down in the field of sunflowers,
did you see that one, too? I in theory rule
exactly one five billionth of the world, up above the paper.
The subject is separated from the object, its verb
hundreds of times more powerful than Milton's God.
The space in between fills with explicit images of Adam and Eve,
    acting as if they had no names, and here we are.

THE FAMILY OF MAN

Hey I know one: The proper study of mankind is what?
Why is there money, Daddy? And why is there daddy, Money?
What is the proper study of Lu Xun?
Guns are made of what? Food is made of what?
Or aren't these the right questions?
Why did Odysseus lose all his men and then kill two hundred more
    when he got home? To stay human?

What happens when you mix five billion people with a lot of cheap
    explosives and real needs?
More at eleven. To gain power
I use reason. To fine-tune reason, I use force, and force's better half,
money, and as a last resort, their child, charisma.

The President was at home giving a speech lesson to his family, the
    nation.
A person at home is at the height of reason.
There are no waves or ticks or hurricanes to trouble reflection,
and the mirrors stretch to infinity. If he were wearing pajamas,
it would be positively Kantian.

Whatever I say is my language, is *in* my language, how do you say, in
    my language they say it like this.
But surely the houses are the same, the horses, the hoses, you use the
    same straight lines, the body divides into the same number of parts,
    the waves, the wives, you have to go to the dentist, the podiatrist.
    One hundred dollars to the podiatrist, and two hundred dollars to
    the dentist because I have more teeth.
I also have more military prowess and am more reasonable.
What do you say to *that*, Mr. Dead Suitor?

What do you say when the epic's over,
you're in your pjs giving a speech to the family,
and the epic machinery is covering the ground so densely that it
    obscures the children's fantasy and determines what they will and
    won't wear?

Are straight lines the same there? Boxes
hold just as much, but it has a stranger flavor.
The dances are different, the music, the sounds, the food, the parasites.

HERE

I'm rolling over, I've fallen out of bed,
what I write you read, without so much as an *is*
in between. First question (sirens blasting away):
Where are we?

"This seems to be an inhabitable planet,
the conditions are perfect for pastoral or industrial park,
let me get a reading on the temperature . . ."
But that guy's on TV, and his costume would make Napoleon blush.

It is well known that there are no final surfaces in dreams,
walking on water turns out to be
a play on words, and waking up
it's somewhere else.

The Federal Building says Federal Building on the outside,
a syllogism masquerading as a tautology.
There's a certain crudeness in lashing the sea, or naming it,
or being emperor in somebody else's brain.

There is no way satisfaction will occur outside of all the bodies of
     everyone who lives here,
and here, also, are the keys to New York City and all the people who
     live *there*,
and to San Salvador and all the bodies in the basement of the Federal
     Building *there*.

I'm not asleep.
Surrealism is was the last gasp of unitary logic,
the single *I* writing the big double word,
but the Mystic Writing Pad was is mad as hell,
it's not going to lie flat and scarred any more.

Captain Kirk pronounces judgment: "Cooling, cool, cold,
a life is wax. A singular stylus would be good.
But there's only so much time to write,
whether you like your costume or even have one."

There's a moon tonight (one narrative
fits all), and private property
patches together a public network of dreaming citizens,
or however we want to designate,
asleep precisely (pardon the religious mathematicity, the lined city,
     parceled out and heaved up into crowded cancer hatcheries), asleep
     precisely nowhere,
where body meets word.

EITHER/AND

My deepest secret but not my weight or credit rating.
The not-I burns the daycare center somewhere near the edge of the
    non-example in northern Nicaragua because pity has a premodern
    ten-year-old face with a hundred and eight handpainted freckles.
My repetition but not my death.
It was either staying home with the baby or a new car. So it was back
    to teaching kindergarten.

It was either throwing sand in theory at my father and spanking him
then astride his corpse to set foot in the sky—wipe that test pattern off
    your face young man!—
finally to sing what came out of my mouth, soberly,
successful as a dream with a replay button
and plenty of money, because you can't have an inner life without
    money, see I'm shy and my words are naked, memory is a private
    blood bank, no AIDS or nasty surprises when you look down at
    your arms in forty years by the light of the stern one-time personal
    law here where the credit flows like air over a soft and living
    landscape, out of many, one and a cast of thousands, the *Me* all
    mine and *Yous* to go!

When this is all over I want to transcribe the Well-Tempered Clavier
    for garden hose, paper airplane, and apricot tree.

There's no guarantee of identity,
which I can say again, but the second time
is under the sad reign of desire:
chairs, tables, vibrators, VCR's, personal submissions,
there's no identity in what it's possible to say
and once it is said
then some historical force, some person
will come edit it, can it, ending with reason and nation, radiating from
    a single scene where we can go home again and again, the wife with
    open arms running up, hair bouncing in slow motion, the kids
    tenderly tracked, the dog speaking non-standard English and not
    eating meat, whatever, it could be anything at this point, the secret
    shimmering on the surface.

FORMALISM

To make a stone stony to make
a shopping center like a shopping center,
these are tasks for a personal person
with an extra world to go to when this one
breaks, or looks too real to change.

To make a poem poetic to animate
the living to count to the number given
by the act of counting, three always
after two, eighty after seventy-nine
has been achieved, lived, stolen
from the silent land where highway connects
with highway and where money-like consciousness registers,
changes hands into instruments of analysis,
breaking public noise into pieces,
ministering to the private fantasy,
but I'm not going to tell you what it is!

To make Grandpa Jack stony
leaving the small stones lying
unmentioned in the narrative.

To write in the printed book—we're mad as hell, etc.—
to read onto the unwritten page—we're made as Pintos, rhinestones—
the idea that something else that isn't an idea is there,
as opposed to millions of pictures of grapefruits pressed excitingly on
    cue into millions of faces simultaneously, Commodity tamed by
    Owner.

But people like watching grapefruits shoved onto unobtainable faces.
There's not always much else that seems possible to accomplish
in any given thirty-second segment of the glistening, elongated body
    of the television day,
though it stands apart and rages, always on cue, like Godzilla, history's
    spare part.

And the single consumer is asked to contain need enough
to tame that body, shoot its imagined strength off the electric towers
    and major buildings. This will require jets, an industrial base, cadres
    of researchers, a trained and entertained workforce, a division into
    sexes, hot tamales and poker faces,
thus accounting, in the twisted logic of the past-turned-present-
    turned-person-turned-face, for the twisted logic itself:
they *have* to say those lines to get paid,
thus accounting for all those half grapefruits.

PSYCHO

If there's no plot, no description, no significant tension of grammar,
    no sex—
but I did just see the primal scene enacted by flies—
then what's in it for my other?
Lived experienced is the answer,
mother I carry around in my basement in the greatest most inward
    movie of all time, all space.

I'm about to lay bare the soul of my device. So flat?
I'm about to globe my thoughts in commodities
soaking up the future making it mine all mine.
Then I'll have lunch, then I'll swat flies.

Now we are awake, he would say,
but she would already have made breakfast, done the dishes, and left
    the house.
Now we change the world, it would say, in Old Slavonic
or, now we change our minds, in the vernacular, in Valleytalk,
but I would already have closed the book and gone shopping.

In the 20s telephones and cars were adjuncts to the self.
In the 30s they were taken away in sufficient number to revive fears of
    commodity-castration.
In the 40s they were used for war.
In the 50s they were given back, but only to Gary Grant.

States of mind enter history naked
but I would already be thinking of something else, other.
It started as a play on words, a casual dalliance with memory,
but ended with a private mind deciphering unheard melodies, racing
    past in an ambulance with mother's ghost solemnly reminding you
    to put up your sword and *use words*.
But it's too late: Gary Grant is dead.
So put away your notepad and hang up your private mind.

Final image: "With the abrupt disappearance of Odysseus, the eternal
    husband, the false suitors disappear. *Exeunt simulacra*,"
leaving a lot of blood to wash off the floors and walls,
which are just a screen memory
shown to convince the viewers of the truth of their suit
and to absolve the spectacle of hiding
a criminal past, primal matter.

APPETITE

All the natural impulses,
like buying low and selling high or calling for your pipe and bowl or
    baking blackbirds on a rainy day,
leave a bad taste. Time only makes sense
chopped into lengths, but somebody has to do the chopping, which is
    not fun, and then they take up space.

Money is the soul of reason, the only way to connect
the shoe factory with the shoe, not to mention the jogger.
And the only way for the shoe
to get outside the box is for money to change hands.

Before, the story runs, there was only an island, palms, sand, streams,
    caves, cannibals,
all waiting for a reasonable person to pay them or pay for them.
Because it's not reasonable to eat people.

The classic cannibal menus remain, with their tales
of sacrifice and preservation techniques. They have no calories
but that works out, because reason is never hungry,
and so reads effortlessly.
Matter is a lazy susan, if you've got arms
and are willing to use them.

The shine on the waves is part of a natural impulse
to mistake light for reason, and both for a healthy diet.
Food is just something to talk around.
A dollar's a dollar, and the world is one interchangeable hieroglyph,
so that one thing means any other, and your birth is your funeral.

Nature has a rhythm, like a busy signal, which is only reasonable,
since words evolved via specific chemicals, which are still in place,
while we, their senders and receivers, are not these chemicals.
Which makes for problems when we go to eat the products of reason.

THE DRUNKEN VOTE

Relentless—as they say—for I am they and I say what they say
(relent, repent, for your or my attention span grows short,
even as the faces and accents on TV accumulate around the ever more
    tired hero, leaping under the car to avoid the gunfire, while over the
    street the brains of the outfit has another sex-like meeting, above
    the stresses of reference and committee striation, where soft rock
    words conglomerate and take on the interminable appearance of
    fate—one second is forever in this language—threshed out beneath
    the starry unsocialized billboards)
relentless, I say, just because I want to and
woke up today, because it was in
my interminable head, cargo cult of consciousness,
I, the broken tribal unity,
worship what goes on above, product
of so many enjambed hands and hours,

relentless witness,
wetness. I want to say
vs. I do say. And today's my day
in court. Holding out the carrot
to the little dog who writes something like a monkey with a human
word habit, a bag of pictures,
each word worth a thousand more words
that the reader, cast in role of detective or rabbi or no-nonsense
    consumer,
has to puzzle out to make a social whole.
Little time remains for saying what you want, which isn't yet in words,
plus there's the physical weight of the problem.

So, what? a relentlessly
sentimental vocabulary of animal parts?
Playing Lassie or the Terminator one last time?
A picture of a satisfied human being
is worth a couple of thousand animal years
of farmlike worship of pure urban presence at sea on the open market
    drinking salt water to keep from drowning down where the
    products stop feeling for you as a private unit of consumption

Hey the rennetless witness has fallen asleep again.
Nor are the TV shows in the TV chairs at the Greyhound station jelling.

Here, by the garage door, in the dispersing scenery,
by the consomméed images of Homer, Tonto, and the nameless face
    on the dollar,
by the triumph of George Will,
smoky light shining down on the torch of freedom held up by the tone
    of solemn curiosity in Barbara Walter's leading questions,
I solemnly swear to inhabit my body,
and having sworn, in league now with fate to the terms of my oath,
on the way back to store,
for I have forgotten something,
I drink the blood of the world, by accident.

ON THE WAY TO THE AIRPORT

The bourgeoisie may frighten away the red, white, and grey dawn
by a live and let live attitude, not that anyone in particular—that arch
    bourgeois—knows who the bourgeoisie are anymore anyway.
History, if it exists, must be embodied,
say in the photogenic Rorschach entrepreneur who sold you your first
    symbol—and how could I forget that exam I slept through every
    night in the train station, it was outside my field, I was the blind
    man describing the moon to the deaf examiner while the taxi meter
    moaned toward extinction—
but everyone has these problems.

After all, the question of class never applies to individuals.
And no matter how hard you press
your intellect against the file photos of demonstrations,
you'll never find any individuals.

One jet goes up, and a few billion people
sink an inch lower, the social surface polished to an exquisite
    slipperiness.
You can't see it unless you know it's there
and if you do, you have to disqualify yourself from the judgment of
    eternity, all you see are misaligned analogies directing every
    revolution to the storefront mirror,
people yoked together by the same money that science uses to sell itself
    its results,
the force at a distance that leaves all hands clean
to drive the car, the career, the graduated class, the heat-seeking
    pleasure-substitute, forward.
So that *this* mighty grain of sand, shirt open at the waist—what's
    wrong with that?—
avoids not one single flake of flame in the heroic sortie
through which idea proves superior, by a few thousand feet, to matter.

POLITICS

Once there was a straight line which told how it got bent.
Someone died and the town was named:
Pittsburgh, Piedmont, Emeryville.
The tree was planted and then cut down,
its leaves scattered by the magic hand of chance.
Now drugstores and hospitals
go through their days, with a profit to show at year's end.
A twelve-thousand-ton building at dusk adopts a certain realistic tone
that metaphors, archaisms, and plain old schizophrenia just can't
    budge.

Chance is a modern idea.
A page out of the book of dreams
can't be just any page, it has to be the very page
where your mother first noticed your father.
They lived in the middle ages, when the sword was still stuck fast in
    the stone and there was no distinction between God and wealth.
There was no time to be subtle: in the ambulance
the Queen of Hearts noticed the Page of Hearts
thus making him the King of Hearts.
But *you*, you nameless blush,
aren't even conceived yet and so aren't supposed to be there
reading, imagining all the names might mean.

There are examples of people overcoming chance,
achieving political embodiment, the posters suddenly materializing,
    ascending to the heaven of free air time, the pure paranoia of
    unendable meaning,
thus gaining a status quite unlike the local hardware store, which
    might in a few months become a jogging store.

Suddenly I heard the car across the street call my name
and so I knew that this was my cue:
as I was saying, once there was a road
that never curved except to provide a bit of pleasure,
but here we are already at the hospital.

LINES

With all the history behind me,
warriors priests concubines dressed in antique skins,
having killed the animals and housebroken the plants,
educated the servants and farmed out the children
—sorry, that was someone else,
not me, who, when I exist, exist atop
a pyramid of past lives,
with all of history under me,
wearing no-nonsense clothes and employing non-nonsense words,
as I enter the description. (See the dollar bill for details.)

But there's no way to parody money.

These ceaseless parodies vs.
the stockmarket, the weather, the kill count
on the front page vs. the kill count on the back page
vs. the kill count not on any page at all,
just in the air, variations of Love Canal,
she's taking an awfully long time getting undressed,
weaving that tapestry, raising those willful children,
counting those votes, delivering those raw materials,
let's apply a little pressure. The ceaseless advance
speaks, murmurs hypnagogically, walking towards the cardboard cliffs
    over which thousands of tiny Tom Swifts, Indiana Jones parodically
    tumble and squeak, spilling into whatever's not history.

A cow chews peacefully over to the side
and milk runs placidly through the cityscape.
Rhetoric tips up and meaning funnels down.
Just a little rhythm and the future begins to appear.

You can make up your own life
with scissors, others,
the bruised fragility of space, the parody of the one thing at a time
    unstoppered sensorium spread to the corners of the most real body
    you've ever seen a picture of

From the live edges of the representative dollar,
the milk deliveries sound, the paper trucks unload, at 7 A.M. the heavy
    machinery, while throughout the morning glimpses of the
    Goodyear blimp float quietly on high

This isn't eternity, have I said that yet?

NOVEL

The law tells a story,
the same one each time.
What happened was this.
It was 1848. The boy's mother
was dead, his father
was absent and as for where
the money came from, the walls
of the rambling house
were silent.
Naturally he was sick.
His own body was always there,
slowing down each minute.
He was in the mood
for lessons, infinitely hard,
with no grades, no way
of passing, standing before
a curious gate locked tight.
There would be no end,
because this was the present.
For instance those mullions,
painted white, the same size,
identical in shape, separated
in space, a fugue a sheep
might have written. This is not
my language, and this is
not my world. Every moment
of my life is a lesson,
he felt, grabbing onto his aching
leg as it passed by
in time, and I want
to be buried next to my mother
but nobody knows where she is.
It was 1898.

While he grimaced under
the weight of the gridded plot,
the bulk of the story
was shouldered by the girl,
a commonsense outsider,
the forces of population
beating stolidly in her veins,
but repressed by her drab
exterior, whose desires
had been driven into strategies
of neutrality in the governess's presence
and of furtive solitary exploration.
The governess was disgusted as the girl
displayed the stigmata of history
in the little chip of the family tree
she carried around on her shoulder.
For the reader, of course, this chip
was all that remained of home.
But point of view becomes
a touchy subject when history
has made you some designated letters
a quarter inch high
with no place to go but inward.
So it was crucial for the plot
and for whatever commercial success
the plot aimed at that this chip
not be knocked off. If it fell,
time would shatter
into hundreds of smalltime
broadcast outlets, each
releasing assortments of mutually
threatening stories. Identification
would go up in smoke.
And so, though narrative *is* annoying,
better a certain amount
of pain, pruning, blushing unseen,
uprooting, thought the governess,
who never would live
in her own book, she
would be the first to admit it,

nobody got to,
that was the point, better
a unified time and a single ending
reached via the gorgeous secret
garden where the mother was
buried, names of flowers
springing brightly from the page
anticipatory as an afterthought
in a cyclical universe
where the girl's humiliations
would be justified while she
blushed in her wedding white
to music dictated by the general
idea of progression, logic
in its marketable form.
But under market conditions written
desire is not free
to simply flow downhill,
that is, the girl's not going to get
to the end unmarked
by some lesson driven
over her and even when she is
shown receiving the world the plot
turns out to owe her,
the force of the embrace
as her husband enfolds her in the center
of a system of ancient hedges
and gorgeous smelling views where
the help are feudal but spunky
and have interesting accents,
the kiss that bestows this on her
has such momentum that the chip
she's been carrying so long
gets knocked clean off her shoulder,
it shatters, evaporates—no matter,
metaphors turn out to be
just domestic tools, like dustpans
or sponges—and now she
is behaving like a person
whose life is already over,

which it is, as the perfect shade
of social space watches
itself close over her.
So the story does
break, there's no room
in it anymore, the headlines remain
untranslatable. The last we see
of her she's planning her vacation
and writing her will
as she stares at the calendar
in the same kitchen
where she was first introduced to us,
pale, smudged, disgusted, non-sexual.
She's a mother now,
May 1, 1948, ruddy and full,
but her days of becoming
have faded. Color plates of
landscapes, drugstores and airports
fill the remaining pages.

The boy though seems happier.
He runs, man-like, for the first time
into the garden, not generic
but exemplary, shouting, "I can run," the ballast
of a healthy body inheriting rhetoric
at its most primal. Again,
the fresh air is proverbial.
Birds, squirrels, blossoms, breezes
displayed prominently make one
as one reads a completed being
for the first and last time.
It's the present.
The man sees a cardinal on a branch.
The shadows the leaves throw
are perfect, and perfectly still.

CLIPPINGS

    R   = Restaurant
    E   = Equipment
    D   = Distribution,
If you know what they mean,
things make sense.
    So = South
    We = West
    To = Township.

Big Mac $1.64
Large fries .67
Shake $.95
The mirror beneath the menu
shows what we look like
without names.

If the world exists
in its present form,
then if I return the videotape
at 6:10, I owe an additional $2.50.
Before 6:00 I can watch it
as often as I want, driving
the price of each viewing
below the threshold of pain.

The heroes are busy
clearing the stage for the aria,
editing the woman's slashed cheek
into a rising rate of return,
pronouncing the dead center
of the language while looking
the camera so straight in the eye
no audience can avoid understanding
exactly what is being said.

An opera is not exactly a
military exercise but it's close.
Some seduce while others stand out

in the rain singing comically,
accents, bodies, wants
on display. Don Giovanni
waves his weapon furiously
at the gordian knots of parliamentary syntax,
trying to carve the pie into a single piece.
For this he goes to hell,
but now, all things being equal
as the curtain falls, the pie exists
spectacularly, like never before, memorized,
a pre-incarnation of wide-spread pleasure, a
smoothly running machine whose parts
meshing more and more perfectly
will finally taste like the real thing.

The story ends, but remains attached
to something outside itself:
the need of the industrial plant,
flowering and dying in art deco layers,
filling bodies with the raw materials
of desire. The spots on her coat
immaculately unsystematic,
Bambi's legs spread, all four of them,
as she (he?) slides helplessly to the rich,
pristine forest carpet, the eyes drawn
wide in perplexity.

"Do I have to *fuck* you?"
the picture asks the wall,
but the wall, increasingly structured
solely for the display of art,
gets paid to turn a deaf ear
to questions like that.

On the technological side of the page,
silence, exile, and cunning
form, in the famous mind,
an endless web of association
that the reader (the hero
under the horizon) shouldn't expect

to spend less than a decade savoring.
The connections are free, effortless,
because it's always, in literary time,
the night before Christmas,
a long night perhaps,
while outside, in secular space,
the cars with their
self-referential headlights
stumble, and fall in gridlocked masses.
If that's rhythm—an absolute category—
then I'm Santa Claus, contingent and historical,
♫♪ "which nobody can deny," speaking personally,
all alone, in numbers.

Noisy, living at home, addicted
to the obvious, any voice,
in order to stay on,
builds its original colors
out of what's there:
a chilled fork
or a rock
picked up and articulated
by a living hand,
or today's date, July
4, 1987, a little forced
but still apocalyptic.

On July 5, 1987 I wrote,
"The bedrock of the modern mind
is the machine," knowing
the word "modern" referred
to the 1950s at the latest and that
there were no machines then
in the contemporary sense.

That makes this
"psychology," except that word
only occurs naturally
in large introductory classes
where the lecturer floats

beneath the vocabulary
in that weightless way
in which I call words forth here
only to find them a bit recalcitrant,
not equal to the fluid dynamics
of capital, and fatally contaminated
by politics, now that
the present has finally
disentangled itself
from the past.

"Politics" is another word
whose use poses problems
for the natural reader,
because to be placed into circulation
it entails a synopsis
of whatever movie I just saw
on TV, in this case *Hot Rods From Hell*.
This is the poetic act,
the poem being formed from the scission
of the self where its imaginary total
shatters in real time as it meets
its alienated social material
and sits ejected from eternity viewing
the narrative of its salvation
as told to a country for whom
daily life requires a
motionless world as a backdrop
and a never-ending description
pronounced by actors whose wage scales
are all that's left of history.
Space limitations and prior genre commitments
forbid me from entering into
or leaving it: just as
the paterfamilias with the bad back
found his enterprise blocked
by the crowd of three surly punks
that no script could stop,
no talent, no wardrobe, nothing
but a fast car embedded

in repetitive clips of fast car noise
and fast car desert panoramas racing past.
When he wasn't fleeing them
with a grimace that only an immediate
family member could fear and hope
to thaw, he stayed in bed
having his overly-present flesh
massaged by the mother,
a vagina dentata tamed
by Miltown and centuries of epic directors
who could only shoot
while facing the mouth of Hell
and could only face
said mouth fully armored.

This may be obvious now,
but in 1987 the obvious
had sagged so low
as to be indistinguishable
from the media—blurred
modalities all over the place
(it was always to be referred to
as one place, laws were
rammed through, wars were fought,
fractional lives dangled
beneath the whole numbers
in the headlines, a master's
final absent glance held
the institution of art frozen)—
and thus the obvious lay
beneath hard-packed
floors of words over which flowed
institutional paychecks that worked
better than repression, any day.

But staring me in the face
—a figure of speech if there ever was one—
is my confident erotic pen
suffusing its organism with acceptance
of its products and lowering

the critical threshold
until mechanically reproduced
barbarous commonplaces vote
with their feet flooding
the borders and drowning out
the more realized phrases
that were to live on with sufficient
room into the present-like future
contemplated and contemplating
as history would bestow on them
a syntax whose every adjustment would yield
meaning (matching
frame and paper not included).

"Better dead than read."
The book review spoke to the universe
at large in the mirror
about the book absent in theory
or syntax or language, whatever,
the audience given no choice
but to laugh or go stand in the corner.
If, by the casual uprightness
of my prose, I state that we
live here, what I am
propping up is real estate values,
isn't it? as the sun sinks in color,
and the typeface attends
the legibility of desire
in the privacy of Town House Acres,
whose hot tubs the Eskimos
with their hitherto exquisite bruises
are fated to one day invade.
Which is why
I can let you have this one
for under a hundred thousand.

On the right magazine page
this stanza would be worth
a used car door or new headrest,
uninstalled. Words are traces

of wars and wars are classrooms
where the apolitical are taught
the human sciences in a pure exhibition
of how knowledge is transmitted
between capitals.

This is the way
empires end, not with signs
in the sky, but overused
bluebooks. Sunrise and sunset
leave acrid scrawls above freeways
where resumés and police records
of under and over achievers
become a tangle of motiveless presence.
Blue Angels fly over San Francisco
to say TERRORISTS GO HOME.

Not just anybody can
be here now, only those
for whom location and time
coincide in a goodnatured
systematic cultivation of perception
and will. The credit terms
are oceanic like you wouldn't believe
unless you were already there
seeing them, surrounded
by the unbroken linguistic surface
that guarantees certainty while perhaps
foreclosing your future, or
Costa Rica's present, but these
are just terms,
undentable expressions of a healthy
fulltime infinity, which can combine
these raw materials into
jumping off points around the globe
to stage projections of force,
framed statements ready
at a moment's notice. You leave
your irony at home
when you board those planes.

In the morning I thought
as a child, at lunch
I was hungry and ate
what I had to,
in the evening I slept like a top,
my life story revolving
at real time speed, who am I?
asked the nation in the privacy
of the opinion segment of the news.
For if all products flow
marketward, but the market
increasingly is overseas,
bombed, undisciplined, ethnic,
selfish, impulsive, garlicky,
then when I attempt to be
myself, reasoned the nation,
eating a hotdog at the
intersection of science and metabolism,
in a world where gravity
has let me down without an accent
on center court, then my thoughts
—tanks, pigs, spare parts—
must be lined up and enforced.

In my village surveillance
is a thing of the past.
There's no need to look.
A strong motionless light
trained on each from birth
turns the world specifically
into a number of candles
plus one to grow on, muggy sidewalk
and a tree for memory,
as green and heavy
as necessary. One is
alone and mobile.
Private languages which don't really
exist proclaim in absentia
whatever Shakespeare or Milne
or Lenny Bruce they can remember

in the talons of the singular voice
of public space.
Hey you! I say to the H-bomb.
Hey you! *Miami Vice* says to me.

Down the tree-lined
invention of perspective
masses of machines
follow their instincts.
On either side, the stores,
neither virgin nor whore
and with more personality
than either, flesh out
the lines of sight.
The machines are all
man, sexual difference personified,
then empowered past reason's
melting moods, liquid
capital that drips
over the hard covers of
lives willing to be novels
but never chosen, such
is the solitariness
of the heroic genre
inside the male machine.
Just beyond the vanishing point of the headlines
a hundred and sixty miners
come out of a pit.
It's elsewhere the sequence
of numbers on the bills
is verified. Closing my eyes
in silence doesn't change that.

Don't get me wrong.
It's great that words
have meanings, and butterflies
have wings, and people have
jobs, and sovereign nations
have sovereignty. The sky
is universal, the flag

pulls itself up by its bootstraps
to show up against it
and stand in for it.

Nor does the neutral
space of art give
birth to anything
except itself and that
only once. In the teens
it had wanted to die,
just to see what that was like.
A life can be very moving
if it's not yours, just a
darkened spectator and a
pulsing ocean
mano a mano.
But is there a body on the screen
or not? Five bucks says yes
because adrenaline
shouldn't come cheap.

The sculptor making love
to a statue is no less natural
than a face reading
a financial instrument. Chassis
have their pecking orders that
when disturbed become marching orders
at the drop of a mylar glove
or the lowering of an already even voice.
"You're gonna *colonize* me?"
Breathless Costa Rica whispered this,
on her own black beach one day,
July 8, 1987. Chronology
is the soul of fiction, and fiction
gets us where we would have been,
if not for the contradictions
in the naked arms of raw material.

To keep the storyboards
true to life, and to maintain

a minimum of decorum, an outhouse
in every firefight, the CIA
was thoroughly and truly unleashed
in an orchestration
of chance that even John Cage
would have to call deliberate.
Beneath the archaic torso
of voting patterns and viewing habits
the present has left a blank.
It reads: "Moderation for the few
(who must—one at a time—
change their lives),
termination for those chickens
who try to cross the road."
If that leaves out human agency,
like they—inhuman non-agents—say,
just call it realism's
protective coloring.
But a syntax that bombs its own debris
is a syntax that has got to go.

Men words and weapons
have been spent freely and lie buried
in the free market. The dictionary
at the root of this largesse
has love in its heart and a ranch
in each ally. Though it's not exactly
a dictionary or a ranch, more
a nest of airstrips and a set
of tacit understandings, and besides,
it's already shredded,
like words written on water.
It's not to drink.
No need to be literal,
or even use words. The monument
has only a base, carved
in stone from flesh by a bloody knife
with no handle or blade, sharper
than every strategy except hunger.

MOVIE

History is not a sentence,
but this is. And though history
is a word, what it names
isn't. And though I'm a person
who puts words next to
recognizable scenes where
your entertainment dollar
is hard at work, and I understand
there's only so much anyone
can put up with in any given
sentence, still there can be no
straight lines in this mass
of air representing itself
visually as broken into pieces,
temporally as a single car ride
with a unified driver, following
the machine's nose. The landscape
is placed sentimentally on either side
to make the view visceral, poplars,
a starry night, crows over a wheat field,
all engraved in an edible
freeze frame called
taste, that worldly shrine
coextensive with its financial backing
where everything is above average
and the weather gets past the cloakroom
only in the form of haircuts.
It's the pure part, the whole thing,
the last word first, once, and forever.
History is a sob story
that should have known better
except that its head is always being
removed and placed—just this
once, the better to
address you with, my dear—here.
About suffering we are therefore
wrong, the neo-masters, as we use
money to display art,

then write off the money
that mounted the display
in the first place, the only place
in the sun that counts,
up to one and then
it stops, its shade
cool & pleasing, its death
always a story told
—to someone who's not dead, of course.
But if the present is either
eternal or false, like
Tycho Brahe's silver nose,
then what about the calendar,
standing there, a self-
contingent fiction, hands
on hips wide for child-bearing, yet
slim as a jockey's, too, in
a display of semantic undecidability
that American-century language can only
suffer through in a silent
automatic display of arbitrary
displacements. Icarus fell
into the sea long ago. His suffering
is over. His father, the general
whose grandson was born deformed
by Agent Orange, says he would
do it over again. His suffering
is displaced onto the only remaining
figure, the peasant ploughing
in the foreground, just above
the bottom of the frame, the
virile threshold where visibility
stops and deniability starts.
So then grammar *is*
one big evangelical conspiratorial
set of embedding procedures
on top of which certain pleasures
crow to their father in heaven
while far below people get
burned, blown away, or compressed

into expostulations of gratitude.
To call this a language
flies in the face of all fictions
wearing the pre-Raphaelite
cloth-of-gold togas
under which, in every case, beats
the same modernist heart, also of gold,
with an improvised mythic
history on its left sleeve
(so uniform is the power of grammar).
But you have to start somewhere.
What we ordinarily say when
an airplane is flying overhead
is that, though we are not
on board, people are, and thus
collectivisms ground the forms
and directions of every event. If
the particular plane is dropping
white phosphorus do we then
exercise our option to begin
to initiate the process of
disinvestment from whatever name
is painted on the fuselage?
A bit slow for the power grid
automatic as electronic relay
tinged with the smell of xerox
rising from the certainty that
the sun would never have to set
if you own enough, and the night
in which all communists are
theatrically black
could be rolled back to the other side
of the world where it belongs
because of my earnest face, voice,
and illimitable earning power.
The art of governing, using
the obvious to state the monstrous
—but monsters are human, too—
begins by separating the names
of the countries from the people

who live there. The family
is then placed in the sky,
between the transmission towers
and the individual antenna. So that
mother's not dead, she's only
a picture, feeding me pictures
of what it is to be full.
This nothingness, taken off
the truck and wrapped in plastic,
and weighed, labeled, and priced,
has to have come from somewhere, though,
or else I'm an autonomous phenomenon
and in fact, God. But when a spider
the size of a period
tried to garner some flat dead beetle
as big as a grain of rice
the body, that had been hanging
by some thread, fell.
(Sorry to be taking up space
acting out the vacuity of description
in an antiterrorist program
aimed directly at the senses.)
This happened, fated, on July 11,
1987, the past hermetically sealed
from the present by the obsessive
cries of "I was there, I saw
what was given, plus what I took
by right of need," as the calendar,
a Salome of classic proportions
was stripping it seemed like forever,
while out in the alkaline foyer
of the family ranch the H-bomb
stage-whispered, "I want
to start over," wearing a corset
straight out of the Restoration,
such is the interference of time
with thought's straightahead appetite.
The result is a continuous need
to defend what are called
our needs aching for a clean

language because no word
once spoken, launched without
warning through the fence of the teeth,
can be called back without
getting dirty in another's mouth given
the puritan imperative under which
we still live, trusting
in God to back our money up
with that clutch of arrows
in his right claw
and those words, immutable
and humbling, over which
blurring life histories pour,
straining to keep the sense
single and the biography straight,
all the time floating
down page towards the apocalypse
where silent surface crumples
abruptly to noise. No more
cool grey monuments where A =
A, ironically perhaps, but with a thin,
deferred, café-like openness
and portable charm. Political
one-time individual animals
of the free world, born free
and paying at all points
to see the movie, it is you
I satirize with my death's head
outnumbering the camera's gaze
by one when the sun shines,
two when the rain falls heavily
on the thick-slated memory-laden
roofs of past centuries by mistake,
regrettable error, inconsolable
recall. Facts still obtrude
smog-stained facades too modular
to serve as faces, too stressed
by the forced yesses of the building trades
to pass for art, behind which
public turns private

for only dollars and hours
a day. The meter never stops.
There are, right now,
if I can use
such a barbarously out of date
formula, at least ninety covert
ops being carried out (of course
in the passive voice) beneath
the global visibility of what
the meter shows as merely the
fair price. The unconscious
seems highly armed these days
and to whom do I owe this
articulated dread if not to
the structures of defense
resting permanently on their
freshly killed enemy. But to biologize
these conflicts is always a mistake.
The pathos of the dying transformer-like
termite defending its hill on
Channel 9 to music that remembers
the Alamo if not the *Aeneid*
leads directly to the ice cream
and the hand held spoon as
stylus of the self that would
sprout leaves and wings and rule
the world even in its sleep,
heavy and fully formal.
Not that anybody's anybody's
slave, mind you. Just don't eat
so much ice cream is all.
These days are as fresh and
uninfluenced as a new pack
at a blackjack table in Vegas
so why do I think chance
has blood under its rug
and lives in a white house?
On July 13, 1987 I just happened
to see an osprey carrying a
small fish in its talons.

Which is not a detective story,
marching backwards to the scene of the crime,
the moment of the proper name,
the murder, known, sensed
in process, the undifferentiated place
where subject and object merge,
warm and unborn. The reader
whose mind has been excited
by the even steps of narration
to an ecstatic acceptance of
unworked time, the golden age,
is prudently to sidestep
identification with either the
dead body or the revealed killer.
But when weapons proliferate
in their pure, pro-life
state, a unique ending for every
person, then thrillers become the public
vehicle of choice, terror and glistening
threats of pain shown
as near as the senses.
Afterwards, there's traffic, the
bad marriage whose second honeymoon
is such an endless bomb.
But at least the luxurious
falsity of the leaves on
Route 3 is real enough.
My eyes, raised and lowered
in the age of mechanical reproduction,
produce the show that by definition
can never play in the capital,
since it has no acts
and the book is so open
as to be illegible in public.
Then do I think that words
are really neat, that empty
clorox bottles and star wars manifestos
can keep the dew of alien
dogs off my property? But if
they don't speak the language

even in our own backyard
where in a classic coincidence
the Augean stables revolt
with soap-opera-like regularity
though the cleansing procedures
are untelevisable, then why
is Ollie North said to be
so popular? "I used to wipe
his bottom," marvels a quoted
woman, printed in a kindly light
because a user-friendly oligarchy
really wouldn't hurt circulation
when it's underground, with
weather and traffic on top,
shopping. Consumer choice is now
a church, hands lifted upward
to the shelves, striving to work
free of the curse of original
childhood eating habits.
The idea of the green party
sleeps furiously, and because dreams
can only be televised
one at a time, election results
haven't stopped many bulldozers.
But you can't sell a view
without slamming a few heads
into a few facades.
Odd, how easy the news-like
voice comes over and says,
"I am the agenda,
for reasons which must remain
unconscious as cars acting out
the look of a secure self
whose national habits
have been dictated by the ineffable
mouth of a pre-fabricated history."
But neither do I want to press myself
down onto some woodsy center stage,
or feel myself up frugally
beside a terrifyingly cute pond

picking out the loose feathers
to make myself a down pillow.
Threateningly anthropomorphic, I know
what happened next: Cary Grant definitely
walked out of his house, the movie
was in color, a glorious day,
yellow sun pouring in
under the out of focus green leaves.
What did you expect? You don't
have to say everything exactly
when you've lived here for
centuries and can address
generalized experience
while self-encapsulating the ear
as "you." Down the street,
a firecracker went off
inside a garbage can. It was the
Fourth of July, garbage day, and July
14, 1987, all rolled into one
swaggering twinkle, the copyright
of an eye that looked out
over its entire life
with a happy willingness
to be filmed, truly,
anthropomorphically, at home.
Everyone in the theater
knows the plot from here:
Cary Grant was married
to Katherine Hepburn, a woman
who thought Derrida was an idiot
and repulsed his obscure advances
whenever he came on the screen.
But behind Grant's face and its
European-savage-tamed-by-American-
money smile (movies elongate
the eternal sensual present
of all adjectives) lay a nasty mortgage
as big and secret
as the reversed letters in Freud's
middle name. So Grant had to

in fact rent Derrida a room
in his own home, which, however,
Derrida actually owned, and thus
it was Derrida's, not Grant's, bathtub
that Hepburn reposed offcamera in
(don't even *think* of looking there),
talking about removing ticks from dogs
and recipes for making flan.
And it was Derrida, shockingly enough,
whose arm reached in when she
asked for a towel. If Grant tried
to calm her down and talk to Derrida
about leaving, Derrida would merely
suggest that he read them the book
he was working on, which the audience
knew from bitter experience if not birth,
they'd paid five bucks
for a short escape from the taste of it,
the book was really nothing but
the unbreakable mortgage which
would have them out on the street
clothed but cloned, cold and
improperly sexed in the dark.
Brows knit, Grant was forced
to come up with a plan:
he went to work, which
in his case meant buying
a newspaper—the corporation,
not the physical instance—and struggling
against appearances (at this point
the movie loses all touch with
its conventions). At the office
there's a beautiful secretary,
but she's so rightwing she always thinks
she's playing football. Grant is
tempted (he's always tempted,
and yields instantly, that's his charm
but also what got him into
trouble with Derrida).
And soon we see him

crouching down like a quarterback
behind the secretary with his hands
patient and puritanical
under her butt as she's spread
in a three-point stance. This
is the messy part, but apparently
for many husbands in shoulderpads
who only stand and wait,
it vibrates a lot of contradictions
at once. Another deeper rationale
is that in this posture
they represent enough desire
for one, shared between two,
subject and object, proving
that in a world of scarcity
where repression is overabundant
the value of internal restraint
becomes incalculable, while
attending to neurological
sensation becomes more and more
an anachronous luxury.
A nation is a person
(and if an utterly clothed
Cary Grant doesn't convince you
of this all by himself, then
walk naked into the socialist
future with your body
the only badge of realism),
and a nation never dies,
except in the past
or by accident, though sometimes
its processes of reproduction
aren't all that pretty.
So she snaps the ball to Grant
who, though he loves his wife,
has to take it, because inside it are
four-color pictures packed
in freeze-dried prose that prove
Derrida's summer home is
in fact a gulag in Nicaragua,

with lines of people waiting
for buses, for sugar, for paper.
That night, when Grant comes home
with the ball under his arm
the smile on his face means the climax
has begun. Derrida, who senses
the storm brewing, takes out
his manuscript and starts to speak.
But now, thanks to Grant's
sexualized, oppressive and glamorous
hard work at the office,
rather than being out in the cold,
Grant and Hepburn rise knowingly
and retire to the bedroom
offcamera, to the accompaniment of
Derrida's droning nuptials.
The movie has scarcely ended
and already I can hear the cries
of "Focus!" The viewers have to face
something the movie doesn't: continuity
after the end. Nicaragua's still
hanging by sensate threads.
And if presidents still have
charisma, it means that the viewers
have been on hold so long
they they've started to, if not
live there, then camp out, sleep
in cars, or under mortgages
inconstant as clouds.
It's like critics opening
three books at once and writing
"vertiginous" somewhere near
the end of the introductory paragraph.
By now, one day after Bastille Day,
young turks under erasure will
always already have sprung up to
the cry of "Gentlemen, start
proclaiming the due date
of the master narrative in
your sepulchral verbs." Meanwhile, inside

the Bastille itself, spectrally re-erected
for the occasion by his own
Herculean labors, Céline passes by his
phantasm and has it say, "I
am the Jew," which of course
lets him reply, "I am
Céline." In a gap that seems
to have lasted two thousand years
but really only began
around 1848, they stare, frozen
into a horrific equality,
though the royalties,
humiliatingly tiny as they are,
still only flow toward
the one with the proper name.
But while these pathos-ridden
biographical black boxes take
excellently horrifying pictures
of the economic earth mother
with arms folded over
her breasts, fox fur
around her shoulders and
the head dangling down
toward the pit of her stomach
as she crouches in her den
beside the stone age midden
that yawns beneath the urban
job market, such authorial pinholes
are merely the formally
empty sign of the copyrighted
grave of the father.
The trademark sticks up,
disgusting and compelling, and
the record goes round.
The stable author is the hard
needle, and the record is the
moving landscape flying its
nostalgic date like a red
flag towards which the self,
tethered to a dying technology,

flings itself under the semi-
permanent gaze of grammar.
July 16, 1987 the frozen
actuarial laughter vibrates
my pointed nicked head to sound out:
dismantle your nuclear missiles,
bombs, howitzer shells, chemical weapons,
nerve gas, gentlemen, stop
your reactors now, let your loans
float out to sea. And to show
how realistic the present tense can be,
I want to make room in it for
the nightmarish echoes such baby-hard
demands excite: swollen
with the balked, slipped passage of time
and opportunities for pleasure
that were forced to go to
dancing school on their own
graves, comes the whispered
thunder of It's not polite
to point It's not realistic
to point It's not effective.
Tears are running down
the clown's face in the
painting above the motel TV
but framing will get you nowhere
outside the frame. "I
call it the schizophrenic
theory, Bob, if we can
make the reader believe that
any word can come next . . ."
where any word refers to
the nuclear bombs Nixon wanted
to have Vietnam believe
he was willing to drop on them
if they didn't stop defending
themselves. As Sade wrote, "The strong
individual merely expresses
in action what he has received
from nature: his violence is pure.

It is the defensive vengeance
of the weak that tries
to name us criminals."
Another way of putting this,
although it costs a couple
of hundred thousand and takes
up to four days to shoot,
is "We don't know you,
but we love you,"
as the large hands, cupped,
visible only as perfect focus,
reach down to shelter
the fragile but wise,
ethnic but cute children. Good
poets steal, bad ones
watch TV, tears
smearing their whiteface
as they display the verbal
equivalent of scars and apply
for grants five months late
each time. But I mean that
to mean its opposite
in a common space
beyond the required reading
of anthologized eternities
where capitalized, footnotable
obstructions like Ollie North—was he
the fat one or the thin one?—
will have stopped bunching
sound into such clots
of powerless fantasy.
But it's July 18, 1987 and
75 degrees. Some things
never change. The past, for
instance, or the present,
that codes and throws down
its dictates a bit faster than the organs
can ingest, detoxify, and classify them.
But since these organs only
exist in the present and,

anyway, levels of toxicity
are set by the producers
of the poisons, this news
shouldn't be taken directly
to heart or allowed in
to your tea if you're nursing.
The liver's relation to coffee
can be expressed in an
equation if you're nervous
or a news account if you're
tired and irritable. The Kenyan's
relation to coffee is closer
to home and so is usually kept
at an untouchable distance.
But do we at least agree
that the human body is paradise
and that the United States
of America is not?
Of course, until history stops
clearing its so-called throat
and starts speaking in understandable
sentences, such hypothetical constructs
as the human body have
only a very limited value.
But description has its uses
even when you're glued
to the tube and model airplanes
are invading your liver.
They arrive slowly
and are deafeningly cute
as they encapsulate
the vestigial childhoods of males
from Rotten to Reagan.
It was more important
than anything in his life
could have been up to then:
if he could get the decals on
absolutely straight it would lead
eventually to a career
in broadcasting and the private

satisfaction of looking back
on the tortuous wake
of one's adolescence pointing
inexorably to the bouquet
of microphones before one's solitary
mouth with the tangle of
cords leading away to the
provinces, Des Moines, Birmingham,
that one can finally leave behind.
To get rid of the past
and be triumphantly attached
to the present by insulated
maternal cords which one
has mastered with one's
trademarked voice which is only
speaking for others, really—
no wonder the boy whose decals
are crooked sobs so hard
there's no thought of talking.
He's lost his chance
of never needing to know
what day it is, or what
city he's in. From now on
it's July 19, 1987 and
there continue to be invasions
and you can't blame them
on the date or the
crooked decals. For two
thousand years poets have been
promising that the emperor's
son is going to turn
the calendar back to one
while the readers, when they're
not attending to formal
state readings, sit staring
at the subtext of
their clock radios. People continue
to die miserably from the lack
of news to be found
there, too, doctor,

every day, as the display
changes a nine to a ten.
Examples can be multiplied
to infinity without adding
up to the great governmental
one which regards all
attempts to establish nondependent
systems of numeration as
so many slaps in the face
of personified free time
and the free world,
where freedom is the same
as the presence of the
agents of that unity.
The airplane is empty (a shy,
self-effacing signifier)
and can carry anything,
this is all there is to know
under the freedom of
information act, and more,
really, than it's good for you
to know, under our way
of life (you can say
system, and you can gather
numbers, but it's my newspaper
and I can stay as anecdotal
as I feel like.) The rubble
down the street or south
of the border makes
a convenient boundary before which
any story, to be
a story, must come to a stop.
Out of bounds a few
billion people interrogated daily
by the black and green faces
on the money have to wonder where
those unseen small tight visages
are really planning to put them.
Don't mess with fate
or me, the clock radio

broadcasts, all the centuries are
balanced precariously above us
and can come tumbling down
in a few minutes. But any
realism begins and ends
with its appliances.
Wider claims ultimately depend
on the credit of the audience.
Institutions are made
of matter, as the date observes
its static progress. The theatrical
inevitability of that procession,
beefeaters parading in the dusk,
players who've put up
the numbers being inducted
into the hall, is the
pure gold of the visible
truth. The cardboard, corrugated
tin, and concrete under which
people take shelter from the economic
elements are simply the untrue
static of the leaden age
before reception is to be
perfected. No wonder sound
is so unreliable and our bodies
seem so mismatched. One hears
her mother calling, one hears
his father inviting him to dinner
in heaven that very day.
The audience sees a statue
drag the hero to hell
from which only sequels
return night after night.
Grant and Hepburn have not
emerged from that bedroom,
nor will they ever.
That makes
anomalies of us all,
doesn't it?

VIRTUAL REALITY

It was past four when we
found our feet lifted above our

accelerators, only touching them at intervals.
Inside, our car radios were displaying

the body of our song, marked
with static from Pacific storms. Outside

was the setting for the story
of our life: Route 80 near

Emeryville—fence, frontage road, bay, hills,
billboards changing every couple of months.

It was the present—there was
nothing to contradict this—but it

seemed stopped short, a careless afterthought,
with the background impossible to keep

in focus. We weren't pleased with
the choices, words or stations, and

our desire pouted in the corners
of our song, where it clung

self-consciously to the rhythm-fill or bass
or the scratch in the voice

as it pushed the big moments
of the lyrics over the hump.

We were stacked up and our
path was jammed negotiation for every

forward foot. Hope of automatic writing,
of turning the wheel freely in

a narrative of convincing possibility, was
only a byproduct of the fallen

leaves lifted in the ads and
drifting sideways in slow motion as

the BMW cornered away from us
at forty. We were recording everything,

but the unlabeled cassettes were spilling
over into the footage currently being

shot. This was making the archives
frankly random. A specific request might

yield a county fair displaying its
rows of pleasures: candy apples, Skee-Ball,

two-headed sheep, the Cave Woman. She
looked normal enough, standing in her

Plexiglass cage as the MC spieled:
the startled expedition, capture, scientific analysis.

But suddenly she interrupted him, breaking
her chains, thumping the glass and

grunting, as a holograph of a
gorilla was projected more or less

over her. The MC turned his
mike up and shouted, "We can't

control her!" and the lights went
out, which apparently was the signal

for us to stumble out of
the tent, giggling, every hour on

the hour, gypped certainly, but possibly
a bit nostalgic. We had already

fashioned nooses out of coded nursery
twine to help the newscasters with

their pronunciation, and whipped up stampedes
of ghost dancers from old westerns,

not that we could see them.
If we lived here, in separate

bodies, we'd have been home long
ago, watching the entertainment morsels strip

and hand over everything, and telling
the dog to sit and not

to beg. But the more commands
we gave our body the more

it gaped and clumped together, over-excited
and impossible to do anything with.

We turned to analysis, negotiation, persuasion,
cards on the table, confession, surrender.

But there was no refamiliarizing. Our
machines filled the freeway with names

and desires, hurling aggressively streamlined messages
toward a future that seemed restless,

barely interested. We could almost see
our hands seizing towers, chains, dealerships,

the structures that drew the maps,
but there was no time to

read them, only to react, as
the global information net had become

obsessed with our body's every move,
spasm, twitch, smashing at it with

videotaped sticks, validating it, urging instant
credit, free getaways, passionate replacement offers.

THE MARGINALIZATION OF POETRY

If poems are eternal occasions, then
the pre-eternal context for the following

was a panel on "The Marginalization
of Poetry" at the American Comp.

Lit. Conference in San Diego, on
February 8, 1991, at 2:30 P.M.:

_____

"The Marginalization of Poetry"—it almost
goes without saying. Jack Spicer wrote,

"No one listens to poetry," but
the question then becomes, who is

Jack Spicer? Poets for whom he
matters would know, and their poems

would be written in a world
in which that line was heard,

though they'd scarcely refer to it.
Quoting or imitating another poet's line

is not benign, though at times
the practice can look like flattery.

In the regions of academic discourse,
the patterns of production and circulation

are different. There, it—again—goes
without saying that words, names, terms

are repeatable: citation is the prime
index of power. Strikingly original language

is not the point; the degree
to which a phrase or sentence

fits into a multiplicity of contexts
determines how influential it will be.

"The Marginalization of Poetry": the words
themselves display the dominant *lingua franca*

of the academic disciplines and, conversely,
the abject object status of poetry:

it's hard to think of any
poem where the word "marginalization" occurs.

It is being used here, but
this may or may not be

a poem: the couplets of six
word lines don't establish an audible

rhythm; perhaps they aren't, to use
the Calvinist mercantile metaphor, "earning" their

right to exist in their present
form—is this a line break

or am I simply chopping up
ineradicable prose? But to defend this

(poem) from its own attack, I'll
say that both the flush left

and irregular right margins constantly loom
as significant events, often interrupting what

I thought I was about to
write and making me write something

else entirely. Even though I'm going
back and rewriting, the problem still

reappears every six words. So this,
and every poem, is a marginal

work in a quite literal sense.
Prose poems are another matter: but

since they identify themselves as poems
through style and publication context, they

become a marginal subset of poetry,
in other words, doubly marginal. Now

of course I'm slipping back into
the metaphorical sense of marginal which,

however, in an academic context is
the standard sense. The growing mass

of writing on "marginalization" is not
concerned with margins, left or right

—and certainly not with its own.
Yet doesn't the word "marginalization" assume

the existence of some master page
beyond whose justified (and hence invisible)

margins the panoplies of themes, authors,
movements, objects of study exist in

all their colorful, authentic, handlettered marginality?
This master page reflects the functioning

of the profession, where the units
of currency are variously denominated prose:

the paper, the article, the book.
All critical prose can be seen

as elongated, smooth-edged rectangles of writing,
the sequences of words chopped into

arbitrary lines by the typesetter (Ruth
in tears amid the alien corn),

and into pages by publishing processes.
This violent smoothness is the visible

sign of the writer's submission to
norms of technological reproduction. "Submission" is

not quite the right word, though:
the finesse of the printing indicates

that the author has shares in
the power of the technocratic grid;

just as the citations and footnotes
in articles and university press books

are emblems of professional inclusion. But
hasn't the picture become a bit

binary? Aren't there some distinctions to
be drawn? Do I really want

to invoke Lukacs's "antinomies of bourgeois
thought," where rather than a conceptually

pure science that purchases its purity
at the cost of an irrational

and hence foul subject matter we
have the analogous odd couple of

a centralized, professionalized, cross-referenced criticism studying
marginalized, inspired (i.e., amateur), singular poetries?

Do I really want to lump
The Closing of the American Mind,

Walter Jackson Bate's biography of Keats,
and *Anti-Oedipus* together and oppose them

to any poem which happens to
be written in lines? Doesn't this

essentialize poetry in a big way?
Certainly some poetry is thoroughly opposed

to prose and does depend on
the precise way it's scored onto

the page: beyond their eccentric margins,
both Olson's *Maximus Poems* and Pound's

Cantos tend, as they progress, toward
the pictoral and gestural: in Pound

the Chinese ideograms, musical scores, hieroglyphs,
heart, diamond, club, and spade emblems,

little drawings of the moon and
of the winnowing tray of fate;

or those pages late in *Maximus*
where the orientation of the lines

spirals more than 360 degrees—one
spiraling page is reproduced in holograph.

These sections are immune to standardizing
media: to quote them you need

a photocopier not a word processor.
Similarly, the work of some writers

associated with the Language movement avoids
standardized typographical grids and is as

self-specific as possible: Robert Grenier's *Sentences*,
a box of 500 poems printed

on notecards, or his recent holograph
work, often scrawled; the variable leading

and irregular margins of Larry Eigner's
poems; Susan Howe's writing which uses

the page like a canvas—from
these one could extrapolate a poetry

where publication would be a demonstration
of singularity approximating a neo-Platonic vanishing

point, anticipated by Russian Futurist handcolored
books—Khlebnikov once read *The Temptation*

of Saint Anthony burning each page
for light to read the next—

Such an extrapolation would be inaccurate
as regards the writers I've mentioned,

and certainly creates a distorted picture
of the Language movement, some of

whose members write very much for
a if not the public. But

still there's another grain of false
truth to my Manichean model of

a prosy command-center of criticism and
unique bivouacs on the poetic margins

so I'll keep this binary in
focus for another spate of couplets.

Parallel to such self-defined poetry, there's
been a tendency in some criticism

to valorize if not fetishize the
unrepeatable writing processes of the masters

—Gabler's *Ulysses* where the drama of
Joyce's writing mind becomes the shrine

of a critical edition; the facsimile
of Pound's editing-creation of what became

Eliot's *Waste Land*; the packets into
which Dickinson sewed her poems, where

the sequences possibly embody a higher
order; the notebooks in which Stein

and Toklas conversed in pencil: these
can make works like "Lifting Belly"

seem like an interchange between bodily
writers or writerly bodies in bed.

The feeling that three's a crowd
there is called up and canceled

by the print's intimacy and tact.
In all these cases, the unfathomable

particularity of the author's mind, body,
and writing situation is the illegible

icon of reading. But it's time
to dissolve this binary. What about

a work like *Glas*? — hardly a
smooth critical monolith. Doesn't it use

the avant-garde (ancient poetic adjective!) device
of collage more extensively than most

poems? Is it really that different
from, say, *The Cantos*? (Yes. *The*

Cantos's growing incoherence reflects Pound's free-fall
writing situation; Derrida's institutional address is

central. Unlike Pound's, Derrida's cut threads
always reappear farther along.) Nevertheless *Glas*

easily outstrips most contemporary poems in
such "marginal" qualities as undecidability and

indecipherability—not to mention the 4
to 10 margins per page. Compared

to it, these poems look like
samplers upon which are stitched the

hoariest platitudes. Not to wax polemical:
there've been numerous attacks on the

voice poem, the experience poem, the
mostly free-verse descendants of Wordsworth's spots

of time: first-person meditations where the
meaning of life becomes visible after

20 or 30 lines. In its
own world, this poetry is far

from marginal: widely published and taught,
it has established substantial means of

reproducing itself. But with its distrust
of intellectuality (apparently synonymous with overintellectuality)

and its reliance on authenticity as
its basic category of judgment (and

the poems exist primarily to be
judged) (with the award having replaced

aura in the post-canonical era of
literary reproduction), it has become marginal

with respect to the theory-oriented sectors
of the university, the sectors which

have produced such concepts as "marginalization."
As a antidote, let me quote

Glas: "One has to understand that
he is not *himself* before being

Medusa to himself. . . . To be oneself
is to-be-Medusa'd. . . . Dead sure of self. . . .

Self's dead sure biting (death)." Whatever
this might mean, and it's possibly

aggrandizingly post-feminist, man swallowing woman, nevertheless
in its complication of identity it

seems a step toward a more
communal and critical reading and writing

and thus useful. The puns and
citations lubricating Derrida's path, making it

too slippery for all but experienced
cake walkers are not the point.

What I am proposing in these
anti-generic, over-genred couplets is not some

genreless, authorless writing, but a physically
and socially located writing where margins

are not metaphors, and where readers
are not simply there, waiting to

be liberated. Despite its transgression of
local critical decorum, *Glas* is, in

its treatment of the philosophical tradition,
decorous; it is *marginalia*, and the

master page of Hegel is still
Hegel, and Genet is Hegel too.

But a self-critical poetry, minus the
short-circuiting rhetoric of vatic privilege, might

dissolve the antinomies of marginality that
broke Jack Spicer into broken lines.

FROM THE FRONT

This picture can hardly be right:
a man with a hammer upraised

above a grain of sand resting
on a glass table. Then there's

another thing wrong: a scowling man
pushing a baby in a carriage

while across the street a woman
holding a child in one arm

tries the houses, asking for work
on a balmy late fall afternoon.

While I rush through the conventionally
dim 'hallways', 'doors', and of course

up the stern 'stairs' of dreams
searching for the history exam offstage,

the irony of a permanent childhood
uncovers itself and gestures, its markers

falling and streaking all economic surfaces.
The color combinations in the catalogs

wither kaleidoscopically as the market refuses
to open its arms, reveal its

motives, or die in peace. It's
1991—at least it was, once

upon a time—and communism is
dead, leaving capitalism, the word, the

movie, the whole ball of idiomatic
wax, with nowhere to go, nothing

to mean. The free world belongs
in a language museum now, along

with free love and free verse.
In mainstream editorial cartoons Arabs have

big noses and big barrels of
oil, with real and emotional starvation

figured as dunes in a desert
that can't help being so dry.

On the freeways, in malls, in
bed, in couplets, the subjects of

history study, cut class, or flunk,
but no one passes. The soft,

cliched underbelly of consumer desire comes
on screen: the untensed bodies of

money incarnate, generic curls making hay
while the sun shines, the excised

pasts and futures formed into remnant
he*s* or she*s* whose job is

to demonstrate the willing suspension of
economic autonomy. In life, the actors

may be murdered, dead of AIDS
or the recombined by-products of industry,

or have gone back to school,
but nevertheless are there on cassette,

alive and moving, rented and possessed
in the shower with vibrator and

camera eye applied to the place
in the market which stands for

a particularly crude but still undefinable
hope for utopia. No escape from

the implosions of sitting and looking,
or looking away. My little horse

must think it queer. He gives
his harness bells a shake—we

are living in a permanent Christmastime
economy after all; so even if

it hardly snows anymore there are
plenty of harness bells—and suggests,

in a horsey way, that poetry
had better focus on coherent, individualized

spots of time, with a concomitant
narrative frame of loss. A carrot,

in other words, and not theoretical
sticks crashing down on parallel jargon-universes,

with the poet wearing self-critical armor
impossible to visualize, let alone read,

inflicting transpersonal wounds on the microarmies
of intellectuals organized into professional phalanxes.

On the battlefield, discipline is ragged,
and the lines separating the divisions

waver like metaphors on a foggy
spring evening, paired bodies, adolescent, in

love, buoyed on seas of plenty,
articulated by time and energy to

paroxysms of generosity, towards themselves if
no one else. But this is

to lecture the open barn door
well after the flying saucer has

disappeared over the horizon, taking understated
control of the airwaves, leaving behind

the smell of hay, the musty
charm of provincial dress and dialect.

These are the stuff of many
a mini-series, nor do the imaginary

raw materials of this poem-like writing
come from a separate world. The

poet has no job; the only
jobs now involve tracking classes under

glass, the stories accumulating spectacles of
damage. To write the histories with

any accuracy is to write backwards,
true to the falsity of experience.

There are no longer any individuals
or individual poems, only a future

more shattery than ever but still
nearer to us than the present.

Saw chairs back into branches, or
words and actions to that effect.

CHAPTERS OF VERSE

1. There are no poets in the natural order of things.

2. A world in which there are no last names and no families.

3. Each generation comes into existence by its own efforts, not through the sexual activity of its ancestors.

4. The physical present, death, eternity, type.

5. The kineticism of childhood seeks its own salvation behind society's back, in public suffers shipwreck and kitsch.

6. We are the moonlit sea.

7. We beat with thundering hoofs the level limiting conditions of a broadly legible social rhetoric widening itself on all sides, which sees, or thinks it sees, the roof above instantly receding, substance and darkness making up a canopy of shapes and tendencies to shape that shift and vanish, and shortly work less and less, until without effort or motion, the scene lies in perfect view, lifeless as a written book.

8. The scene lies in perfect view.

9. It is only in its resurrection that meaning lives.

10. Subjective workers kiss, not as lawyers, doctors, coast guard cadets, astronomers, sex therapists, or psychic healers.

11. Political language will get nothing but a mixed reception.

12. We, the public, with our dearest domestic ties, adopting our unseen hands as a free ride.

13. Human happiness is an image of relations in blood, binding up the constitution with fashion, melding close impossibilities into a timeless whole.

14. I do not believe poetry and prose will continue seven years longer.

15. When we, the two hundred and fifty million personal poets of the United States of America, have children whom we scarcely know what to do with, we make poets of them.

16. Images in blood.

17. The fact that the poet characterizes poetry as a church leads in a straight line to the founding of a language that goes beyond revolution towards a career of revelation.

18. A glimpse of an apostate son of a Quaker going to sea at sixteen; but the events of his biography lead in a straight line to the resurrection of the activity of his ancestors.

19. Experience is an accumulation of something like capital; but it is always in formation and if it is spent, it leaves the wind and sleety rain, the single sheep, the single tree dead from the wind, the bleak music of the old stone wall, the mist advancing on the intersection of two roads.

20. Uncommon language, loose parasitic body by centralization, acquires a range of daily content and real legibility, not in Utopia, in fields under the earth, or as some secret liberty of bypassing the objective conditions blocking our path, not as textual change in the world. As usual, prostitution is universal, and sacred.

21. There is not enough money to buy all the small-press books. And while there are more than enough diamonds to be the best friends of the eligible singles in the new releases, there are not enough releases to

justify the building of the buildings of a new society. Thus poetry and music limp along like aged friends, against a backdrop of real estate, under a sky of pure speculation.

22. Co-consumers seem perfectly willing to order from a diversity of catalogs. Omni-sectarians of desire ride the continent in search of the appropriate accreditation. Creeds and schools in abeyance.

23. To export need is to speak like a native.

24. Except for single words, there are no objects standing between the poet and revolution, and not just of literature alone, but likewise of society.

25. The poet's mind when writing poetry is a mass of social individuals all using words at different times.

26. Poetry begins, not between individuals within a community, but rather at the points where communities end, at their boundaries, at the points of contact between different communities.

STATE HEADS

We the people, I the person, alive and haunting the discontinuum of
    bodies

Poetry in our time speaks in cars and air conditioners too constant for
    broadcast thought to say more than I see

Let there be headlines and there has to be filler

The President's head, sticking out of the sea on page 2, an absent
    rolling expression on the face, signifying nothing save shutter speed

The sinning son of a sod buster gone and got elected as a concrete
    universal

The President is the current one, the President of electricity, the President of particulate emissions and diamond vision, grass and dust, a motion surrogate dividing the landscape

Underneath the paper split pebbles of commercial nonsense bake in the sun, deleted by a light blue pencil or a dark red pen

Normal usage is the art of channeling weapons so the majority of sentences willingly enforce the current meaning of money with a minimum of state body revealed in the headlines

No sonic boom, more a slow drought and dubbed thought printed tonight and not allowed to age until tomorrow

In public and in fractions, jouissance delivered to responsible individuals

A god's resumé recognized at a glance

Terrorist-consumers struggling to eliminate the single word of slave prose

The poetic reader withers away

Some personal viewpoint tucked well under the freeway overpass with a story to tell and no one but the police to tell it to

Poetry and advertising, boardroom and bedroom, converge in the Wild West of governmental privacy

Jets above financial canyons the real picture of fictive capital

Sense-seeking words rived by career reading

Chernobyl was the kind of joke that makes poetry serious

Go back to the dawn of time, pick up a club and plot revenge, or wake up and smell the freeway burning

MONEY

I am I because my little dog knows me
—Gertrude Stein

Wallace Stevens says Money is a kind of poetry. So I offer to trade him Tennessee, States, and Water Works for Boardwalk and Park Place and the four Railroads. He thinks he'll pass. Do it I say and I'll quote you. Do says he. Mesdames, one might believe that Shelley lies less in the stars than in their earthly wake, since the radiant disclosures that you make are of an eternal vista, manqué and gold and brown, an Italy of the mind, a place of fear before the disorder of the strange, a time in which the poet's politics will rule in a poet's world. Yet that will be a world impossible for poets, who complain and prophesy, in their complaints, and are never of the world in which they live. Yes he says, gorgeous, I'm throwing in Pacific, North Carolina, and Pennsylvania. Go on. I can't I say. But do he says. Fair use I say. But all use is fair to one such as I says he, *continuez*. No I say, 11 lines, any more and I'll have to write to Vintage, which I really don't want to do. But that's nothing he says, 11 lines out of 187. He says I'll give you Marvin Gardens, Ventnor, Atlantic.

That was the present, the poetic present tense: a non-financial play space, overheard.

Money has tenses: it has absolute meaning in the present; no past; and its future meaning (interest rates) reflects the degree to which the future is expected to resemble the present.

Writing has tenses: the past tense makes the most money (novels, reporting); the future is for prophecy (crop forecasts, pennant predictions); the present continually has to borrow credit. I am I because I say so and my little audience knows me.

Wow, says Basket. Wow, wow, wow!

How much money does it cost to know that Basket was a series of dogs owned by Gertrude Stein? Nothing, now.

I give I will give Basket the following bone (all past tense):

There was once a man, a very poor poet, who used to write poems that no one read. One evening, after working all day on an especially poor poem, he fell asleep in despair at the sterility of his imagination and the bleakness of his chances of making it as a writer. He had just typed the lines

The sky was mauve and as far away
as a ten dollar bill.

He awoke with a start. The dim light from a small full moon was shining down at a forty-five degree angle on his hands and the typewriter keyboard. He had slept two or three hours. Instinctively he looked up to the page—it was his last piece of paper—but it was gone. The moon shone on the bare roller.

Then he saw the page beside the typewriter. He must have taken it out before he dozed off, he thought. When he picked it up to put it back in the typewriter he noticed a small slip of paper sliding off the top—money! He stood up and snapped on the light. A real ten dollar bill, green and crisp!

He felt elated. His first reader! A realist who nevertheless appreciated his metaphors or similes or whatever they were! Real money!

Still inspired, the next morning he bought *The Selected Poems of Emily Dickinson* and two pieces of paper. That evening he wrote a careful twenty line poem and went to sleep expectantly.

The next morning: nothing.

He put his last piece of paper in the machine and began a poem. The first line was

The girl took twenty dollars from her mother's purse

followed by 49 more lines describing an approach to sex and the experience of alienation. It ended,

Dew beaded the windshield.

Sure enough, the next morning, there was a twenty dollar bill on the page, and a checkmark next to the final line, which he took to mean "Good."

He went out and bought *Ulysses* and *The Words* and, confidently, a single piece of paper. One was all he would need.

Late in the afternoon, he popped open a Bud and began to type away cheerily. He waited till he was two thirds of the way to the bottom of the page before mentioning the sum of forty dollars, which of course he received the next morning, the two twenties placed neatly on top of the page lying beside the typewriter. There was no checkmark, but he didn't mind so much. He did have a slight headache, from the beer.

Needless to say, he made lots of money. The checkmarks were irregular, and in truth not all that plentiful—many of what he thought of as his best passages remained checkless, while some of the low water marks apparently went over well—but he was pretty stoic about it. He was always paid in cash, even when he mentioned sums in five figures.

One day, when his library was almost complete—he had bought *My Life* and *Vice* that afternoon—he felt a strange stirring in his stomach or teeth or forearms, he couldn't pin it down. He wanted to shop. He grabbed the 1,600 dollars from the night before, stuffed it in his billfold, and went out to find a grocery store and an electronics store: food and TV, why not? He was productive, well off, his work was read. Why not relax?

His first stop was The Good Guys. He had a long talk with the salesman about the makes. It boiled down to Mitsubishi vs. Sony. He was naive but the salesman was there to help. He decided on a Sony. He wasn't going to get remote control, but it was part of the package. How was he going to pay? Cash, he said. He worried that it would draw a funny look, but it didn't. He reached into his pocket, and to his horror the bills he saw in his billfold were Monopoly money: two orange five hundreds, four yellow hundreds, and four blue fifties. He looked at the salesman, whose hair, he noticed, was exceptionally neat.

The poor poet thought of the sheet of white paper waiting for him in the roller. He had been thinking of getting a computer sometime soon but now he just wanted to get out of the store and relate to the somber physicality of the typewriter.

He had already waited a couple of seconds too long to pay. He gave the salesman an orange five hundred. "Where are you parked?" the salesman asked, as he handed the sales slip and the bill to a woman at one of the cash registers. "Oh," said the poet, truly at a loss. "I didn't bring a car." "You can pick it up tomorrow," said the salesman, "just bring your sales slip."

Wow, says Basket, but only one wow.

I ask him about Gertrude. He says she wrote for money, too. Every word.

PRAISE & BLAME

I mean this says the written body a lame duck
a world without money still as a written line

I mean this says the written body a lame duck
market the results or at least publish them

a world without money still as a written line
distribution determines rank a literary word

without a past magazines printed at irregular
intervals don't remind me a constantly broken

market the results or at least publish them
distribution determines rank a literary word

intervals don't remind me a constantly broken
sequence of investments the imperfect tense I

was moving a chair hearing a clock tower ring
without a past magazines printed at irregular

I remember buying but not reading the *Tibetan
Book of the Dead* I've parted my hair the same

place since age ten the original word without
sequence of investments the imperfect tense I

was moving a chair hearing a clock tower ring
echo "younger than spring time" a sentimental

education is always one life too late so that
when the spectacle touches my body I'm slid

into the trench history's an umbrella made of
echo "younger than spring time" a sentimental

place since age ten the original word without
education is always one life too late so that

I remember buying but not reading the *Tibetan*
machines twenty clouds in the sky and all for

naught a problem the non-biodegradable future
will inherit with its characteristically bent

into the trench history's an umbrella made of
sense of purpose the date is grey in grey and

alive in a spread-sheet morgueish way shows of
force torching the human buildings twisted

place since age ten the original word without
depth torching the human buildings twisted

sequence of investments the imperfect tense I
dead satisfaction left never mind the feeling

intervals don't remind me a constantly broken
echo "younger than spring time" a sentimental

victory utter annihilation the body following
circular songs of praise and blame knit tight

force torching the human buildings twisted
into the trench history's an umbrella made of

victory utter annihilation the body following
like a dog children wake in chapter eleven of

the Bhopal Trilogy men from Big Blue ride the
painted wooden helicopters above the hospital

crib no need to render details unto Caesar in
our lifetimes outtakes stand for authenticity

market the results or at least publish them
a world without money still as a written line

victory utter annihilation the body following
like a dog children wake in chapter eleven of

our lifetimes outtakes stand for authenticity
the Bhopal Trilogy men from Big Blue ride the

solemn confusion around the career trajectory
only authority can be present the audience is

free to attend as attendant nutshells dance a
solemn confusion around the career trajectory

shoehorning the credit-worthy fifteen million
into cars the face and the voice copyright in

solemn confusion around the career trajectory
machines twenty clouds in the sky and all for

dead satisfaction left never mind the feeling
painted wooden helicopters above the hospital

a world without money still as a written line
alive in a spread-sheet morgueish way shows of

victory utter annihilation the body following
into cars the face and the voice copyright in

a world without money still as a written line
sense of purpose the date is grey in grey and

I mean this says the written body a lame duck
shoehorning the credit-worthy fifteen million

intervals don't remind me a constantly broken
Book of the Dead I've parted my hair the same

crib no need to render details unto Caesar in
circular songs of praise and blame knit tight

AUTOBIOGRAPHY BY APHORISM

The father was attempting to explain castration. "They say it's completely academic, but believe me, it's not. I'd like you to sit still for a second, not squirm, not plug your ears, or make faces, or keep your face blank either, and please just listen. Don't watch my mouth. This wasn't my idea, either. Just assume a normal expression and maintain it out of courtesy. History doesn't take place in your room, for you to lip synch. Mick Jagger is a symbol of the death of aura. His sweaty face has the farce-fed grandeur of all reruns of authenticity. Every sentence has a subject, whether the sky's on fire, or the kettle is humming its little tune in time to the daffodils. Do you want lift-off or just Brownian motion? One comes after two. Rotate your utopia to line up with my body's time and then we'll be able to skip the past tense in our family wagon—remorse in every western—the problems the Smithsonian has with the color adjustment of multiculturalism so close to the White House. Pick any pebble. Better than Bartok, better than Proust? Remember how we struck gold on the prairie but each grain was so heavy we couldn't even lift our arms to turn off the radio to write America as one word? I gave you your name, and your first word was the sound of a bullet ricocheting. It was still hot at sunset and the air smelled almost like a kitchen. There was a lake in the center of the distance, as concentrated a blue as I ever hope to see. But it was like trying to settle in a giant's hoofprint. I hope you're writing this down—multiculturalism is one word, Brownian with a capital B. Are you even listening to me?"

> *Extremely happy and extremely unhappy*
> *men are exactly alike.*

The one time I was in Paris I pawned my dictionary for a bronze model guillotine. I only knew one person and my clothes were more unconsciously provincial than I had ever been, which I had always been proud of in a sneaky sort of way. Thought was total. I wrote sonnets: my record was two minutes and forty-five seconds. They rhymed, too. On commercial forays I employed staccato ellipses: des oeuf, pain. If I'd been a dog I probably would have looked for a lamppost. As it was I eked out my niche, and manicured its voids with insurgent symbols. It was the end of the beginning, the dumbshow of the gods, just for me, but since literature is signed by pragmatic rules, I quickly returned to America having written only ampersands for the reader to translate into a present tense.

The writer is the one
who is always the author's favorite.

The milk bottle joke depends upon changed values given to "boy" and "mother." If time never stops, relative to the cultural capital spread across the desk in homely, personalized messes, then incomprehension becomes a kind familial response. Is it that you love your body, or do you just resent any question as to its being? The joke is the kind that brings in secondary characters, education and jobs, big wars which filter into the room and make the desk a place of high-powered consumption: caffeine, endless references. But it was an ill-starred attempt to escape mother, whose ghost brought the most inefficient gossip, every afternoon. He couldn't keep her out. The result was writer's block as we now say, a poor surface on which to scratch out the forms of his inmost desires, not to mention bringing them to careful fruition. Lifetimes later, a statue stands pointing out a grim city dawn, surrounded by detective slasher real estate prose, whose solidified violence forms a track for the laughter that never comes. Morning pronouns comb through the crumbs, but it's too late. Breakfast is over.

There is a great difference
between praise and blame.

If art is to remain heroic, and the nation a place that all young people willingly want to paint & breathe & compost in a serious way, then someone should write a screenplay where John Wayne, played by George Washington, meets W.E.B. Dubois, played by Spike Lee, crossing the Delaware, played by Molly Bloom or James Joyce. The question of who gets to discover what continent and where on each other they might find them would get the plot going and cuts, focus, gesture, and accent could take it from there. Underemployed autosexual ushers would hand the audience walkie-talkies to keep in touch, trade perceptions, and market impressions. Nature would issue its own banknotes. Black and white bodies on the melting icefloes beneath the ozone holes invisible behind the fog—if the theatrical climate could be kept cold enough, the old political narratives could be felt with the clarity of a test-pattern. There would be a heavy circle enclosing the public clash of vested, disembodied interests in the shape of an X or an I or an asterisk, providing a nexus of jobs and a circumference of emotive postures, and nothing else. The action would take place in the winter palaces of the audience's frozen breath.

Most of the world's troubles come
from making a mistake.

The Titanic was a literary theme, Managua is not. Pinched nerves are geopolitical burdens. A man sees a name on a tag. So what's social life for if not changing channels? The movies have taught the viewing class to read a crocodile surging as a natural language. The hero is hardly eaten at all. You can leave the television on, do whatever you want. They can't see you.

Terrorism is essentially the rage
of literati at a banquet

I used to harbor a conception of the self that derived from the day when I was two and looked up at the sky. It was full of clouds, a fleeting composition forming a euphemism for language. From that day (I have a postcard of my point of view framed by vines) I was free from all memorized vocabulary and the consequences of whatever apologies I might utter at school. A pleasure, transposing fate into style without having to worry about the failures in Genesis. A marxist tourguide of the Cataclysm showed me the wind, and where it integrates into factories and then into the stinking creeks. Her analysis was sexual, and I thought it was right to read her thirst for community as inclusive.

Nature never happens twice.

She reaches behind her neck to undo her pearls and habit, willing the moment to sleep. Obedience dreams of pressed precise glyphs, groupings, curves, wakeup calls under sunny trees, a plunge to obsession in the mire, classes where the units strip right down to the White House. But that is all hearsay. Meaning slips into something less natural.

Nothing is more beautiful
than being able to set a bad example.

CHRONIC MEANINGS

for Lee Hickman

The single fact is matter.
Five words can say only.
Black sky at night, reasonably.
I am, the irrational residue.

Blown up chain link fence.
Next morning stronger than ever.
Midnight the pain is almost.
The train seems practically expressive.

A story familiar as a.
Society has broken into bands.
The nineteenth century was sure.
Characters in the withering capital.

The heroic figure straddled the.
The clouds enveloped the tallest.
Tens of thousands of drops.
The monster struggled with Milton.

On our wedding night I.
The sorrow burned deeper than.
Grimly I pursued what violence.
A trap, a catch, a.

Fans stand up, yelling their.
Lights go off in houses.
A fictional look, not quite.
To be able to talk.

The coffee sounds intriguing but.
She put her cards on.
What had been comfortable subjectivity.
The lesson we can each.

Not enough time to thoroughly.
Structure announces structure and takes.
He caught his breath in.
The vista disclosed no immediate.

Alone with a pun in.
The clock face and the.
Rock of ages, a modern.
I think I had better.

Now this particular mall seemed.
The bag of groceries had.
Whether a biographical junkheap or.
In no sense do I.

These fields make me feel.
Mount Rushmore in a sonnet.
Some in the party tried.
So it's not as if.

That always happened until one.
She spread her arms and.
The sky if anything grew.
Which left a lot of.

No one could help it.
I ran farther than I.
That wasn't a good one.
Now put down your pencils.

They won't pull that over.
Standing up to the Empire.
Stop it, screaming in a.
The smell of pine needles.

Economics is not my strong.
Until one of us reads.
I took a breath, then.
The singular heroic vision, unilaterally.

Voices imitate the very words.
Bed was one place where.
A personal life, a toaster.
Memorized experience can't be completely.

The impossibility of the simplest.
So shut the fucking thing.
Now I've gone and put.
But that makes the world.

The point I am trying.
Like a cartoon worm on.
A physical mouth without speech.
If taken to an extreme.

The phone is for someone.
The next second it seemed.
But did that really mean.
Yet Los Angeles is full.

Naturally enough I turn to.
Some things are reversible, some.
You don't have that choice.
I'm going to Jo's for.

Now I've heard everything, he.
One time when I used.
The amount of dissatisfaction involved.
The weather isn't all it's.

You'd think people would have.
Or that they would invent.
At least if the emotional.
The presence of an illusion.

Symbiosis of home and prison.
Then, having become superfluous, time.
One has to give to.
Taste: the first and last.

I remember the look in.
It was the first time.
Some gorgeous swelling feeling that.
Success which owes its fortune.

Come what may it can't.
There are a number of.
But there is only one.
That's why I want to.

A LITERAL TRANSLATION OF VIRGIL'S FOURTH ECLOGUE

Washingtonian[1]

    1. "Sicilian" in the original; in the original-original,
    "Sicelides." "Washingtonian" is an upsidedown synecdoche

    (so to speak): a false-toned part
    of a false whole in the service,

    finally, of something a little less false,
    or so I like to think.

[Washingtonian] Muses, let's roll up our sleaze,[2]

    2. Puns usually announce (denounce) the excess
    of organization in language. This one gestures

    in the opposite direction: it's pretty random.
    It's hard to believe I feel

    compelled to notify people that "Washington
    is sleazy," and certainly there are more

    direct and convincing ways to do that.
    This piece is an inverted pun,

asserting two very different things are identical.
Perhaps the desire to be wrong

is the heart of wanting to write.
There must be some pleasure there.

                    [let's roll up our sleaze,]
and invest in the grandest theme

park of them all: the past,
as basic and embodied as Fess Parker's

coonskin cap.[3]

    3. Do people remember Fess Parker? He played
    Disney's Davy Crockett, America's original libertarian.

                    [Fess Parker's

coonskin cap.] If a man is wearing
another animal's tail on his head

his emotions aren't to be dismissed,
even if his speech sounds like he'll

never finish chewing Ma's final biscuit
enough to swallow it all the way.[4]

    4. I find it odd the way
    'subject matter' (sic) creeps into this writing.

    Somehow the couplets commit me to continuity
    —one could hardly call it narrative;

    the areas of most interest (to me
    anyway) seemingly begin as sideways moments.

    I compare the past to Fess Parker's
    coonskin cap: suddenly like the proverbial

chicken hypnotized by a straight line,
I find myself focusing on Fess Parker.

[to swallow it all the way.]

Never mind his noises, they're only
one of history's running gags: the back

door may creak at midnight, but meanwhile
the whole house has been repossessed.

The feelings in Fess's script are
as difficult to deflect as a hungry

ghost or loan officer. Let the world
remain imperfect food; let the mossy

stream in back of his Tennessee[5]

5. Doesn't Stevens's "Anecdote of The Jar"
—"I placed a jar in Tennessee, / and

round it was, upon a hill"—
anticipate the current Biosphere (the dystopic Eden

where scientists are spending two years in
a sealed-off greenhouse)? But "Tennessee" doesn't

say this, without my overdetermined reading.
Art, I want to say, saw teeth

rasping at my branch, is not separate.
I can hear those Disney basses

now, those archaic corporate muses, chanting,
♫♫ "Born on a mountain top in Ten-nes-see . . ."

[let the mossy

stream in back of his Tennessee] cabin
choke in a few decades with

the wastes of a single narrowly
chiseled narrative; let each wine-dark tree hide

its Disney savage in defiance of history's
singularity; but this copyrighted archetypal whiskey-drinking

typo-fighting individual—Fess Parker is only
one of his many names—will remain

centered in time's freshly baked diorama.
Now he squints into the sun, watching

the golf ball he's hit halfway
to Singapore disappear into the cloudless sky

to thunderous applause. There is no need
to be anxious over the path

of the ball or over the fate
of this tableau:[6]

> 6. But of course I am anxious.
> Why else the footnotes? I began one
>
> poem years back: "Ed Meese is not
> relentless necessity." Soon (or already perhaps)
>
> I'll have to worry if people know
> the name. Mr. Memory might answer:
>
> "Ed Meese was District Attorney of Oakland,
> California when Ronald Reagan was governor.
>
> When Reagan became President, Meese was
> his Attorney General and had a particularly

partisan sense of duty. He chaired
the Meese Commission on Pornography." This poem

is a reaction to the religious right's
authoritarianism based on transcendent language (the

bumpersticker puts it: "God said it. I
believe it. That settles it."), and

fear of labile pleasure. The poem,
then, is a place of such pleasure?

Counting to six and seven as I
try to clear the ground for

my desire for pleasure?? (Labile, the man
said, make mine labile.) Who is

Mr. Memory? Mr. Memory himself might say:
"I was a character in Hitchcock's

The 39 Steps. An idiot savant, I
could remember phenomenal amounts of data

and was used as a transmission
device by German spies before World War

Two, though without knowing what I was
doing. (You could call me Ion

[from the *Ion* of Plato, where
the rhapsode, the reciter of the Muses's

blueprint is ultimately without knowledge, the merest
conduit]—I feel that I need

to make these things clear. Otherwise—
lability. Also, if you'll remember the movie,

I couldn't help but spew facts
when asked.) After some decades of writing,

there comes a point when the contours
of one's verbal habits cease to

surprise. Or is it quite the opposite?
—that a certain doppleganger keeps coming

back, one's own unowned nameless body,
in verbs, vocabulary, linebreaks, no pushing it

away by storms of invention, inventories, concentration,
'the magic hand of chance,' thinking

with the words as they appear,
the dictionary's icestorm lying shattered and bright

in the morning sun you'd think
the inner dome of heaven had fallen

—I had to look that up:
Robert Frost. Who cares! A world without

a ground of repetition is a world
without poetry. I, Mr. Memory—remember?

—died at the end, in cold
Hitchcockian denouement, too fast to seem quite

final at first, and the secret
of the noiseless engine remained hidden inside

my small fictional body. I never talked
anything like this, it's only because

I was asked that I'm forced
to ride the rails of this answer."

[over the fate
of this tableau]: in a few

days (or centuries, it makes no
difference) Fess Parker may be unknown, squeezed

onto a magnetic card of 1950's America
and its actors playing colonial heroes,

his terms as President only remembered
by over- or under-paid specialists, but this

is a prophetic poem, Virgil's 4th eclogue,[7]

    7. Christian thinkers considered Virgil's 4th eclogue
    (37 B.C.) a prophecy of Christ's birth.

                    [Virgil's 4th eclogue,]
and the principal attribute of such

canonical utterance is its perpetual freshness.
Time stands still and meaning is everywhere.[8]

    8. I like it when the couplets
    come out even. (Assuming 13 is even.)

    (But how to imagine a poem touching
    a specific time many centuries later?)

[Time stands still and meaning is everywhere.]

It's shocking but true: I'm translating literally;[9]

    9. I'd thought about claiming this was
    a literal translation a few hours ago.

    Half-thoughts were flitting about happily in single-winged
    narcissistic swoops in the half-lit belfry:

I would quote the Latin. Push irony
to its ecstatic death in lie.

At tibi prima, puer, nullo munuscula cultu
errantis hederas passim cum baccare tellus

which my eye fell upon just now
by chance would be good because

of its structure of one seven word
and one six word line, like

these couplets. I wanted to say
that the quoted Latin was a translation,

a literal one, from the original
Latin. At one point I half-wanted to

refer to the original printer's error in
Canto XIII, which has since been

corrected without Pound's permission. (When Kenner
pointed it out to him, he dismissed

the problem, saying, Repeat in XIII
sanctioned by time and the author, or

rather first by the author, who
never objects to the typesetter making improvements):

And even I can remember / A day
when historians left blanks in their

/ writings, I mean for things they
didn't know, / But that time seems to

be passing." / I mean for things
they didn't know, / But that time seems

to be passing." If I had
any vocabulary (never mind the knowledge I

guess!—first things first) from computer programming,
I could make specific reference to

something like recursive instructions: the original
Latin would say to quote the original

Latin in the translation. I should acknowledge
the Monty Pythonesque qualities of these

'thoughts'. (That's not to say they're not
original—at least I think they

are.) Burroughs's sense of the word
as virus is hovering in the vicinity.

                         [I'm translating literally;]
in fact, not only are these

Virgil's exact words, the sounds are identical
as well. Reading this, you are

reading the original Latin, a contingency
that I, Virgil, foresaw[10]

  10. At this point, I've decided to try
footnotes as a way to react

to this piece: it feels strange enough
to merit such measures. Perhaps this

equal strangeness will create some balance.
For the record: this was the first

footnote (originally written in prose, though I'm
currently rewriting it in couplets, as

well as adding to it), but
the poem itself mocks origins and records.

[a contingency
that I, Virgil, foresaw as I wrote:]

At tibi prima, puer, nullo, munuscula cultu
errantis hederas passim cum baccare tellus

as well as its rough translation—
But to you, first, child, little gifts

from the uncultivated earth, wandering-about ivy
with its berries (perhaps a hint there

in baccare of Bacchus and state power
torn apart and eaten by orgasmic

women out from under the so-called thumb)—[11]

    11. The violence of oppositional sexuality that
    most authorities fear takes a cornucopia of

    forms—face and voice altered, social
    markers shown as flesh and unanchored expression

    —isn't flesh something that gets *eaten*?
    Chew, grind, tongue the pulp, taste—splashed

    to pieces like a visual stick
    in water at the moment the bodies

    become, as Harlequin romances like to write,
    "one"—but the violence of state

    sexuality is the oneness of that oneness,
    mythic marriage with all the trimmings

    —Bush opposing the species diversification treaty,
    saying in the Fess-Parker-gone-to-college accent that if

they think I'm going to do anything
to hurt the American family . . . is

it always state eyes that stare
at Miss March photogenically licking Miss April

and the invisible hand of the marketplace
that rubs its thumb and forefinger

together with only the glossy paper
intervening? Looking out of the poem's eternally

framing open window at this week's
breaking glass, I see our nation, pinnacled

atop its past: Macedonia, Rome, England, Cambodia
—remember those pyramids of intellectual skulls?

                    [orgasmic

women out from under the so-called thumb) —]
This has been written already in

the original because, with the birth
of the ruling child[12]

12. There's a crucial possibility open here:
I'm really tempted to write ruling-class child.

The eclogue can certainly be read
as an egregious piece of flattery: Virgil

owes his leisure to Maecenas, Augustus's
minister of culture more or less; this

dependence leads him to write the *Aeneid*
as an epic in the service

of state power, transmogrifying Homer's oral-based
aristocratic-communal technique into the protocol for imperial

pedagogy and angst for isolate authors.
The fourth eclogue is often preposterous under

the strain of laying utopic pleasantries
at the feet of a state official

(Pollio, apparently) who has just become
a father. I.e.: This is the ultimate

age foretold by the Sibyl's prophecy . . .
the Golden Age returns . . . it's while you,

Anne Imelda Radice, are consul that
this holy age begins. Everything will happen

a second time: Theseus will sail again
for the golden fleece, movable type

will be invented, we'll know what
it means this time. The child will

live a godlike life, and see
the gods . . . he'll rule a world

pacified by his father's virtue. . . . Goats will walk
home untended with full udders, oxen

no longer fear lions, snakes will die . . .
the ram will dye his own

fleece now yellow, now purple, grazing lambs
willingly shall turn their wool red,

you won't need your wallet, full-time childcare,
snorkeling, handsome Caribbean waiters smiling beside

roast beef, shrimp and quartered pineapples.
But I respond to the poem, too,

especially the end: Begin, little child,
recognize your mother, smile at her, she

underwent ten tedious months, begin, little child:
if you don't smile at your

parents you'll never be worthy of
sharing the feast of a god, or

the bed of a goddess—Freud!
where *were* you when *that* got written!

Despite the sycophancy, the poem has
a charge: pleasure and love are at

the root of the intelligible world,
and the potentialities that flow from that

are just and beatific. That happiness
animates Virgil's conditional claim near the end:

if the utmost of life was available
to him, and if he could

sing the fact of this child
with sufficient inspiration, then he would be

a better poet than either Apollo
or Pan: that's an interesting human claim.

                         [with the birth
of the ruling child,] time becomes circular.

That circle has been completed in footnote
12, letting me step outside to

these words I wrote thirteen years ago:
Steal a few moments from the

running time Max shoving himself against
the netting of his playpen finds himself

his bottle now standing on the back
of his busybox toppled twice now

standing stooping down two hands raising
his bottle on high aria furiosa long

notes held searched through some blocks hang
off the railing he puts them

in his mouth and sighs pulls himself
up wooden bead on a string

in his mouth tasted dropped eyed
at arm's length he leans back and

groans at the ceiling chanting pulsing O's
until he begins to jump now

a forefinger in the mouth to chew
and modify the noise waving and

a falsetto yodel picks up spits out
the bottle crawls in a circle

spits picks it up drinks embraces the
basketball and rolls over goes go

go go as he hits his
wooden nails with his hand stands at

the railing going Da da Da
jumping looking over his shoulder short plaintive

hums escaping almost whining he reaches up
to the doorknob on the other

side rattles the door staring up
to the top using his strength jumping

talking a brief emphatic silence then
a yell he turns away then sits

walks across the mess to this side
again begins pulling up the mat

staring at the fiberboard underneath a few
glissando squeals now some O's as

he stares at and touches the metal
tube brace standing again feels the

shiny chrome bolts at the top
hangs down by his arms head back

up to the ceiling he almost falls
over swings sideways does fall down

cries his bottle's stuck between the webbing
and the floor he gets it

out drinks deep breathing hard holds it
at arm's length bangs his fallen

busybox drinks again stares at and fingers
the nipple a moment of quiet

while he farts backs away squeals
spits goes yay grabs it drinks throws

it down spits propeller noise from
his lips stares at me pulls himself

up standing at the railing on top
of his busybox falsetto yodel now

large modulated calls out to space
staring at his feet as he slides

one along the smooth cardboard back
of the busybox which squeaks he crows

turns it with difficulty back over
picks the thing up hits with it

drops it picks up the pink pig
nailbrush puts it in his mouth.[13]

    13. Imagine writing that would make good
    its second by second letter by letter

    birth and existence as if the body
    moving made spaces it could understand.

THE MANCHURIAN CANDIDATE: A REMAKE

1st shot (for the trailer)

Bang we see the crosshairs targeting
the spineless forehead

2nd shot

Didn't you hear me the first time?
We know you know what we're saying to you.

3rd shot

They have such power over me
but Frank isn't bothered by them all that much.

Ulysses lies there on his floor
a closed block with a big name.

4th shot

Closeup of the dustjacket: words.
They have power over me.

The dustjacket is orange & black
but this is black and white so I just say it.

The cover isn't part of the book—obviously.
I'm not in the movie—obviously.

5th shot (for the trailer)

A harpsichord on the soundtrack signals
something's false—this is the 50s, remember.

On top they're hearty, fussy old ladies;
underneath they're murderous cold war hypnotists.

On top they're discussing hydrangeas; underneath
they make soldiers strangle each other.

On top it's a movie;
on top the frozen war.

Underneath markets wither; underneath
pleasure, all its eggs in one basket, explodes at the sound of shots.

Underneath you have to follow these words to the letter.
You're on top.

6th shot

At last the truth can be told.
Let all the spies stand naked.

I was sitting in the den
watching a tape of *The Manchurian Candidate*,

secular, married, legible, American,
looking at what's showing.

Let all the words be sold at cost.
Let all the words be read at cost.

I was playing solitaire because of Korea.
The deck contained 52 diamond queens.

7th shot

That was in the movie,
but a picture is exactly where I don't want to live.

PANDA—Where would you like to live? China?

KOALA—I'd love to visit. The food, the umbrellas, the bicycles. Where would you like to live? Australia?

PANDA—Australia's too ironic for my taste. I'd love to visit, though. I've never seen a kangaroo. Their leg muscles must be remarkable.

It looked as if I was coming out ahead.
Not quite victory, perhaps,

but what have we been fighting for
all our lives if not

a New York
where you can go into a bar in the fifties,

order a beer and read *Ulysses*?

I saw paradise the other night.
It was as easy to read as breathing
and writing one's invitation to the world
in progress, frank, surprised, very amused.

It was a dream I can't remember
—obviously—in a phrase not this one:

this is just an assertive shielding
echo, a deeply loved surface.
Then I woke up. I was watching television.

8th shot

The clicker and a right hand above grey couch material.

9th shot

The grey voice never transgressing word boundaries,
the plate compartmentalized, the carrot section

filled precisely, never a spatter of pureed orange
slopping into the section for desire,

which was filled with a clear layer
of deeply loved picture:

the blonde biking by tearing off her blouse to bandage his leg
where the snake had conveniently just sunk his admittedly abstract,
    offscreen fangs

—Why not? narrative homeruns
over the abyss of incoherence

are America's
ice cream—

I saw leaden geo-toy Raymond Shaw
murder mother and father
in the snap of the plot;

10th shot

while I was waiting for the kids to go to sleep
so you could nicely slip your underwear off.

Oops you went to sleep.
I never meant any of this.

I have not done these things. Any of these things.
I write for you and strangers.

11th shot

in her bra, outside. Summer.
Some are others.

Not her.
Friendly. Filmy.

12th shot

I place myself in the position of the viewer, then I view.
On the night in question I was home all evening, viewing.

188   from *The Future of Memory* (1998)

13th shot

Frank Sinatra's had it. The social cardboard's
not worth the sweat he constantly carries around on his face.

Wherever he looks:
locked American lives.

No writing the great book.
Might as well read the ashtray.

No loving the great smile, no riding
the city down to bodies

that can be yours for the right song,
the instant aria just before the light changes.

Too many cigarettes,
too many buddies strangling each other.

Why? Because.
Why? Because the smiling Chinese totalizing science sentencer of
    history

pronounced the words, just the pleasantest trace of accent,
"With the hands."

14th shot (for the trailer)

I Chinese view duty-free writing strangle experience
you Amerikanski mister irony door plenty WD-40 but no key poly-sci
    thinker figure out later-never.

15th shot

Frank wasn't strangled but now he can't read *Ulysses*.
It means nothing to him, just another big brick of paper named after
    itself.

When the world is weird,
being bounced around on a word trampoline won't get you any rest.

From in front of the VCR field in the psychic past of the Cold War,
this is Bob Perelman.

16th shot

Yes, mother, every word must count: 6
Yes, father, I will count each word: 7

If any one of them gets away
then I will be alone in

a locked mess. The warm curves
the grassy hills and the actual caves

I will want to write myself.
Please I'll write it myself. The way the streets

look from inside the house,
at night, either end blocked or shielded,

the maple leaves lit black green
by streetlights, stating my feelings of home,

mouth & ear and leading them
out to the attentive spark. I read

Jack Kerouac who is free
to drive a Ford in the specific direction

of heaven where art
is a very good investment,

although you only should say that
well after the fact.

In 1955 the many love the few
or at least the few are free to think that they do

and ♪♪ "it was a very good year,"
the present recording its pleasure in being

recorded. Frank Sinatra is rewarded
with a stage full of panties and keys

while standing up and swaying,
his inward light spotlit smokily,
throat open to extort
every sung syllable,
the bedroom board meeting
smoldering, shareholders on fire,
humming along. In 1955, art is
as exciting as the perfect bid,
the sunsoaked homerun,
the victory over the others
that they like too, acknowledge, buy,
put on the wall.

Kids wait,
but the early offscreen doors don't reopen.

17th shot (voiceover)

The Manchurian Candidate stars Frank Sinatra
as Benny Marco, Lawrence Harvey as

the horrible Raymond Shaw, Janet Leigh
as Benny's girlfriend, Angela Lansbury as

Shaw's mastermind mother. American soldiers are
betrayed in Korea, and captured by

the Chinese Communists. After offscreen brainwashing,
they are shown to the Russians.

Both groups are intellectuals, quoting conflicting
studies as the commonsense Americans sit,

bored but patient, in alternate shots,
brainwashed into thinking they're at a

horticultural meeting in New Jersey where
matrons in white dresses and broad

flowery hats are attending a lecture
extolling scientific gardening. "Another modern discovery

which we owe to the hydrangea
concerns the influence of air drainage

upon plant climate." Slow modern harpsichord
jangles the soundtrack. The film is

racially progressive: when the onscreen American
soldier is black, his hallucinated matrons

are uppermiddleclass black; there's no plantation
subtext. When Shaw is ordered to

strangle another soldier, he's almost too
polite, saying "Excuse me" as he

brushes another's chair; the soldier to
be strangled is polite, too. It's

a liberal utopia: good manners have
triumphed over competition. The Chinese are

jovial and authoritative—they've perfected the
procedure. They can make the Americans

believe anything: the Camels they're smoking
turn out to be yak dung.

It is to laugh, for the
Chinese mastermind at least. The Russians

are surly and badly in need
of dental work. You can't believe

what you see. But you have
to look. Finally, the poem is

beginning to focus. We know you
know what we're saying to you.

KOALA—I hit my head; I had a dream. Isn't that how it always starts?

PANDA—Maybe that's the way it starts in the West. It's not a collective
form; there's no rhetorical place for people to come together. That's
the way you've started, but that's not the way it's supposed to start.
Hitting your head is personal.

KOALA—I was cutting the grass and I hit my head on the branch of an
apple tree. An old one, twenty-five feet tall with two live quarters
sprouting north and south, two dead ones east and west. It was not
symbolism, only matter. If you don't believe me, you can feel the ridge
of healing flesh on my head, under the fur here. It's as real as history.

PANDA—Cutting the grass is a fairly trivial instance upon which to bal-
ance the non-concentric circles of history. Go in, I would have said,
have a little lemonade, & read Whitman or the Misty poets. Particu-
lars only exist by being collective.

KOALA—So the public—fuzzy little me in the case of your remarks—be-
comes crucial.

PANDA—When you're a nation, being cute is not enough any more.
No, a public is a serious, collective enterprise. The ironic single
writer in a cage, treasonous, or loyal, or mad, riven by pathos, unfa-
miliar tears . . . it doesn't really matter much to the words or the
world. Once the hypnosis of the singular is snapped, that is. Before,
one can think that anything might happen on the page.

KOALA—I'm willing to bob for very small favors, balls of hard, candied
poetry swimming almost ethically in the sweat of irony's personal
furnace around which individuals are gathered into gendered masses

in lieu of lives for all lived under the changeable blue fields of utopia otherwise known as international justice!

PANDA—International justice! I think we might as well change the subject, don't you?

KOALA—Fine. Which do you hate more, symbolic poetry, or poetry that's all language?

PANDA—Easy: poetry that's symbolic.

KOALA—But what about poetry that's all language?

PANDA—Poetry that's all language makes me cry when I'm asleep and can't hear the tears hitting the pillow, I mean the page.

KOALA—I actually hit my head: that means something. It was hot, I was one body for the duration, cutting the leaves of grass and I saw myself walking on air on cloud stilts of biological perpetuity and sweat of the word. I was not a nation, I was not a species, I was a speaker, fully alive just because I like the sound of that the noisome hiss of this making a made world under me undergo twisting birth and destruction just to keep me saying what I was going to say anyway! Or anything else! Or nothing so what black hole blank! An apple an unoriginal rhetorical sin a day goes astray into the many minds of the many many others who don't think this! And neither do I! Neither we nor me! Am I allowed to say this? No! I say it! Thanks to the body beyond species, beyond genre, thanks to the dictionary, the strikers, the Haymarket lexicographers! The Tiananmen Square grammarians! I say it! Out loud! Where was I? Where are we? Don't you love the intrusion of speech where no speech can be, life where sounds are the slippery start to never finish but get there already anyway . . .

PANDA—Did you show that to your trainer before you turned it loose on me?

KOALA—My teacher?

PANDA—I'm assuming your teacher was your trainer before he was your teacher.

18th shot

I can't remember the movie anymore.

Art means throwing scraps of code

to the bodies as appetite supplements.

The screen is softwired so the bars disappear.

after the primal shot

I can see eyes painted open
on the death mask of that lovely
arrangement I used to call the world,
America, my life, the page,
the academy of the future,
which, as it turns out,
is in the past. They even move.
They're mine: that was home.

It's plain that there was time
and that it took place
but its quick pleasures are now words
in a language with only scattered survivors.

A single word means nothing.

Or a line without a world.

The present is full of survivors' sentences.
With disoriented conviction and memory
too deep for instrumental speech
swimming sinkingly toward pre-owned futures
hosed down the hyperspace of capital
where freedom spells the rampant logos
turning attractively bemused typefaces and icons
toward the traffic.
Or language it for yourself.
Make your own recipes: ironize,

experiment, write wrong,
but don't forget
the old pleasures:
skies, turkeys, playgrounds.

We know you know.
Meanwhile, one drives,
an open lane a paycheck of sorts,
leading to the autobiography glimpsed
in the gas station john mirror.

During the war there's nothing to eat
but information and denial, the new
mixing with the old
down through all the details. Taste.

19th shot

Who folded my clothes?
You did! I did!

Who watered my tears?
You did! I did!

Who batted an eye each word I woke?
You did! I did!

Who waited for me to sleep so I could wake one step further inside the
    world?
You did! I did!

KOALA—To survive you have to be willing to do anything.
    Anthologies! That's where the money really is, or might be. At least
    so I imagine from my fuzzy animal distance. Reprint the material!
    Dominate the gene pool! Rise like Godzilla and make them read you
    for fucking ever!

PANDA—If you use language like that, you'll have a hard time even
    making it into the La Brea tar pits.

20th shot

To be free and to be
Frank Sinatra the pinnacle artist

but to be pictured as *homo ordinarius*
keeping the public world private

by visible quotidian heroism:
that's the lesson scorching the director's desire

in every shot. If you feel like arguing
with the movies, then step outside.

21st shot

The Chinese mastermind has the one
successful marriage in the movie.
(Yes, it's offscreen: you can't have everything.)

He's really a most happy fella.

We rejoin him as he leaves
the Russian doctor-spy's so-called clinic in NYC
after ordering Shaw to murder
his would-have-been father-in-law, the honest muckraking journalist,
as well as the love-of-his-life blonde.
Don't fall asleep,
this is plot.
Everyone has to sacrifice.

Except for the mastermind perhaps,
jauntily tugging his gloves tight,
saying now he has to get off to Macy's
for some Xmas shopping.
Smiles the happy social smile sans dissonance:
the wife gave him a list yea long,
shrugs: what are you gonna do?

He knows how to get in bed with capital
and let it charm his pants off.
Having them "tight enough
so everyone will want to go to bed with you,"
as Frank O'Hara writes, is a youthful gesture
under the dappled shade of capital's
frond-like pleasances.

That's one thing.
But to live as a large system of control is quite another.

As the mastermind leaves, the Russian stares.
He just doesn't get it:
he believes in history
not Macy's, inexorable direction, totality,
the concrete-translucent materiality of class to classless truth,
one world one history at the end!

Meanwhile one's provisional oneness
stands and waits with oblique conviction
against the waterfall of wage-slaves
—that rainbow spray is guilty as Sunday!
Those sunny lakes, those caves of ice,
those miracles of rare device
forced from the deep romantic chasm
of bourgeois pastoral-pornographic shopping,
which that crypto-individualist Chinese mastermind indulges
with his credit flowing past the respectful cashier
like vodka down a mule's throat!
Or whatever!

Thus the Russian revolutionary-bureaucrat-murderer-actor
placed on the verbal screen
by the all-too-human history of this shot.

closing shot

Shaw's gunsight targets
Communist McCarthyite foster father's forehead,

as said before, though in a novel continuum.

The movie wants to reach the new world
and, in the same gesture,

to conclude. A narrative should hold you
with intimate concern, but not too close

because you'll be heading out one day,
pegged, looking back

for the recognizable trees, the known cars,
glad animal movements traded in
for manageable novelty . . .

Is the nostalgia for creation or destruction,
or for something that hasn't happened yet?

Beside the encrusted place names,
flags of private longing
flutter against the vistas,
and molecular revolutionaries dream of taking all desires to court
and setting them loose beneath the robes of judgment.

To pull the gown from knowledge,
to pull the eye from noon,
and not to see the catered wants
of Tom, Dick, and Harry
navigating the street, the mall, the clicker and the dust!

And Jane, Ketisha, and those tender technocratic shoots and stumps,
you and me?

On screen, nations personify the pursuit of happiness,
tearing families to shreds and the shreds
to costumed certainties of loss and rage.
Beyond the blinds:
the end—rain falling on cue,
Frank Sinatra crying, Janet Leigh wordless.

The days regular as sprocket holes,
while decades slide by
with unevenly layered minds of their own.

You! Hypocrite viewer! With nothing but mirrors
for pleasure, knowledge, luck.
My hand in yours if you read me.
Those deprogrammed people glimmering beyond
the evening's blocky conspiracy theories,
willing their present without shooting our past
to a bloody parable
—have you found a way to call them yet?

CHAIM SOUTINE

I

Unclose your eyes, you look ridiculous,
untip your head, shut your lips.

Listen. I'll tell you a secret.
I learned this when I left the *shtetl*

—that means home town,
everyone's from the *shtetl*. That bottle

you're clutching. In the *shtetl* it's called
the bottle of last things.

Everyone gets one. It's supposed to be
invisible, it's bad luck to mention it, they say.

But take it down from your mouth.
You didn't know you were holding it!

They say that's good luck,
and the tighter you close your eyes the better.

The world in there, all yours:
visions, powers, messiahs.

But now that you know—hoist it back up,
run your tongue around the rim,
feel the glass, if it's beveled smooth,
curl your tongue into the neck,
do whatever. It's yours.

But the big secret is . . .
It's empty! Glug glug!

You've swallowed it all! Tasted good?
Who knows! All gone!

Bottoms up must have been
your very first word!

And guess what that means?
Nothing left! Bad luck!

Finis! Curtains! Triumphal openings, Picasso elbowing over to chat—
nothing, forget it!

I've found out the hard way.
But at least I'm not in that ridiculous posture anymore,
squeezing the neck, eyes screwed shut, piously sucking.

Here's my advice: throw it away.
smash it on the curb,
go heave it through some stained glass.
Just get rid of it! Now:

head level, mouth shut, eyes open,
forward march . . . we're big doomed heroes!

2

God can give you the world
(glug glug!), sacred word, covered ark and all,

I can paint you
pictures of whatever—curtains blowing open,
nice tablecloths, high class space,
sides of meat, streaming red, glistening, clotted yellow.

Push the paint, whip it around.
It likes it. A strip-tease

without the tease and without stopping at the skin.
The girl thinks I want to see her body—

surprise! Keep your clothes on, sweetie,

you're here to wave away flies.
They're actually pretty, patchy fur swarming

over the side of beef if you
let them settle, but it's

much prettier bare.
Keep waving.

Your arms are killing you? So what.
After four days hanging there it doesn't
smell so great?

Hey, my blood didn't taste so great
when the god-fearing neighbors beat me up

in the name of the Almighty.
Thou shalt make no graven images

and thou shalt smash the kid
who tries to paint the Rabbi

and here's one for free
in case anybody forgets what No means.

3

Let's build a frame of common
sense, stating the case with deeply

received ideas and fields of trophies
to hold the still-warm ashes, yes?

What's happening? Soutine, non-verbal painter
of crooked landscapes, people, meat, is speaking,

supposedly, but it can't be, time
is a problem, and place,

one's place in the senses, facts of habit, recognition,
situations where art is produced, carefully broken windows

placed at careful distances
from customers who are always right.

The dramatic monolog is far down on the list
of living forms, supine, disgusting really.

What is an anecdotal Soutine to me,
and what am I to these

acidic bursts of no one's speech

and they to the decomposing composition?
The desire for heroic writing splits

into appetite (glug glug!) and horror
at the achieved sentence (keep waving!),

while the eye (your mind or
mine?) sticks the words like pigs,

with syntax underneath to catch the
flows of meaning. The taste

of lost things is a tyrannical pleasure
and is always in infinite supply.

4

For the sake of art,
modernist coffee, Paris,

it would be nice
to hold some things separate,

let the anxious animal graze outside forever
on museum grass

while, inside, history's waterfall flows upward,
sharp white walls

keeping the vision of taste safe
from the mouth that wants grapes

perpetually bursting into the old original wine:
Make It New.

The Louvre
is the *shtetl* of *shtetls*.

Unless our home
is language, raising us

inside its womb. Reading its shifting glitter
I almost forget I ever learned

to write in half-lit
rooms and blocks and days.
There are lives outside

the correction chambers of this page.
Couldn't it be stronger? Time

to stop and name. Print
on paper for the neighbors.

CONFESSION

Aliens have inhabited my aesthetics for
decades. Really since the early 70s.

Before that I pretty much wrote
as myself, though young. But something

has happened to my memory, my
judgment: apparently, my will has been

affected. That old stuff, the fork
in my head, first home run,

Dad falling out of the car—
I remember the words, but I

can't get back there anymore. I
think they must be screening my

sensations. I'm sure my categories have
been messed with. I look at

the anthologies in the big chains
and campus bookstores, even the small

press opium dens, all those stanzas
against that white space—they just

look like the models in the
catalogs. The models have arms and

legs and a head, the poems
mostly don't, but other than that

it's hard—for me anyway—to
tell them apart. There's the sexy

underwear poem, the sturdy workboot poem
you could wear to a party

in a pinch, the little blaspheming
dress poem. There's variety, you say:

the button-down oxford with offrhymed cuffs.
The epic toga, showing some ancient

ankle, the behold! the world is
changed and finally I'm normal flowing

robe and shorts, the full nude,
the scatter—Yes, I suppose there's

variety, but the looks, those come
on and read me for the

inner you I've locked onto with
my cultural capital sensing device looks!

No thanks, Jay Peterman! No thanks,
"Ordinary Evening in New Haven"! I'm

just waiting for my return ticket
to have any meaning, for those

saucer-shaped clouds to lower! The authorities
deny any visitations—hardly a surprise.

And I myself deny them—think
about it. What could motivate a

group of egg-headed, tentacled, slimier-than-thou aestheticians
with techniques far beyond ours to

visit earth, abduct naive poets, and
inculcate them with otherworldly forms that

are also, if you believe the
tabloids, salacious? And these abductions always

seem to take place in some
provincial setting: isn't that more than

slightly suspicious? Why don't they ever
reveal themselves hovering over some New

York publishing venue? It would be
nice to get some answers here—

we might learn something, about poetry
if nothing else, but I'm not

much help, since I'm an abductee,
at least in theory, though, like

I say, I don't remember much.
But this writing seems pretty normal:

complete sentences; semicolons; yada yada. I
seem to have lost my avant-garde

card in the laundry. They say
that's typical. Well, you'll just have

to use your judgment, earthlings! Judgment,
that's your job! Back to work!

As if you could leave! And
you thought gravity was a problem!

SYMMETRY OF PAST AND FUTURE

The absence of theory has seized the masses
Adorno

Chapter One

OBEDIENT PLIES OF WRITING SO FLEXIBLY THIN THEY'LL SAY ANYTHING. HISTORY GLIMMERS OUT OF A PAST ONE PART REPRIEVE AND TWENTY PARTS EXECUTED DESIRE. IT HIDES IN THE SHAPES. WHAT'S MISSING CENTERS AROUND YOU, LAUNDERED ENCLAVE OF SENSATION, LIBIDINOUS CORPORATION OF BODY PARTS, CRASH-TESTED BY THE LATEST INVOLUNTARY MEMORIES, REFLEXES MUDDLING THROUGH, RETINAS CURVED AROUND THE VANISHING POINT. A SKY FALLEN ONTO THE MORNING PAPER, UNFOLDED TO GIVE TERROR A HUMAN FACE AND SHOW IT IN A POEM. POEM! THE VERY WORD IS A SHTETL PHOTOGRAPHED, ITS ACCENTS REMOVED NOW FROM ALL CHANGE. THE WIND STILL BLOWS FROM THE FUTURE BUT THE ERA OF THE SINGLEHANDED SENTENCE IS NEARING ITS CLOSE. HOW MANY DIVISIONS ARE YOU STANDING IN FRONT OF?

from *The Future of Memory* (1998)

Chapter Two

Where language is, there
    I was once, infant,
        everywhere, held in the
            devices of an enchanter

who smiled, hand over
    heart, pledging perception's daintiest
        favors, far back and
            fast forward. The jailers

are in eternity, too,
    with their pieces of
        cake that have nourished
            our formulas for pleasure

for so long now,
    the past humps up
        until it can only be
            guessed at, tangled in

the bedclothes. Dark morning,
    the whippers burning in
        the sconces, eager for
            a full day's work.

Chapter Three

no ovens
no ships
no showers
no whips

no scalpels
no pliers
no genealogies
no wires

no salt water
no rope
no chairs
no files

no chambers
no gutters
no trenches
no ditches

But we live in a land where the laugh track floods, the candidates rise
above class, ties loose, chests there to be beaten, where the wind
blows free for the first month, after that some charges apply.

Chapter Four

The absence of theory pulses in my neck,
at least I've thought so,
sitting on the edge of the bed, pulling off my socks.
Break the life-mask of empiricism and, underneath, prophecies
become visible: the death of the past, swaddled in
old jargons of self-expression: those other bodies.

The next layer down we find a typewriter,
at least in my case,
the platen nubbled in a grid where the breath habitually roosted.
So you work away, dusting and smashing alteratively,
a kind of rhythmic settling of ever older scores
like an eye sinking into its socket.

Chapter Five

Which reminds me. There was this
South Seas island, and in the

alley, after the shows, they'd gather,
to wait for the stars. So

this one person is there, staring
at the bricks, not really seeing

them, the invisibility of the obvious,
et cetera, etc. In some versions,

they're classes. Class: I met some
of my best friends in class.

And so the one brick says
to the other brick, You ever

see a shrink? And the second
brick says, If I saw a

shrink the whole wall would be
in big trouble. And the first

brick says, I hate to be
the one to break the news,

but you're not that important. And
brick number two says, Touché, and

big deal, too. Touché away all
day, and I'd hardly feel it.

But how about you? Did *you*
ever see a shrink? And the

first brick says, Yes, it so
happens that I did, one time.

I go in there and the
shrink says, You need to find

the inner you, that'll be one
hundred dollars, and I say, You're

kidding, the inner me is in
no way different from the outer

me, if you don't know that
from the get-go then what am

I doing here? Touché, says the
shrink, you're right, it's been a

long day, and you're not my
last brick. And then I say,

Now if you're going to be
asking for my sympathy then you

should be paying me, how about
we make it ninety bucks, because

I'm not one to copy your
material. Ha ha, says the shrink,

but that one I've heard before.
No, what I meant to say

is you've got to find the
real you. Forget inner. Real hooks

up with the material conditions among
which consciousness undergoes its traumas and

desires, and it can lose its
shape, easily. Well, I say, *I've*

heard *that* one before, and it
was in a better version, too.

I mean, "material conditions among which
consciousness"—who do you think is

still listening at that point? You're supposed
to be *helping* people, not getting

it, whatever "it" is, right, whatever
"right" is, so the teacher won't

take out his red pen and
get your paper all bloody.

Chapter Six

Anyway, the way the better version
goes is when you say, That'll

be one hundred dollars, then I
say, When I find the real

me I'll get him to pay
you, and then you're supposed to

say, It's not that simple, — Wait,
how does it go from here?

Ah but that's why you're here,
interrupts the shrink, to get access

to those repressed memories. Then maybe
you can find the real you.

Shut up, I explain, so I
can remember how it goes. You

say, It's not that simple . . . Wait.
Oh yes. Then I say in

answer to that, You're right, who
knows who is who, I don't

know who I am, and you
don't know who I am, I

could be anybody, I could be
you, maybe I owe myself one

hundred dollars, who knows? and maybe
you're me and you owe me

one hundred dollars, who can say,
but I'll tell you what we

can do, let's just split the
difference, you give me fifty and

we can call the whole thing off.

Chapter Seven

Which except for the usual allowances
is pretty much exactly the way

I heard it, says the brick.
And speaking of identity. Once there

was a Jew, a Serb and
a Samoan, in a lightbulb, when

it starts raining, first only a
few drops. But it turns out

that one stands for ten, ten
means a hundred, and then the

uncountable masses of others who maybe
kick your skull around if you

get too close. In some versions
it's a soccer ball. A whistle

blows. You touch my mirror and
boom: Seven centuries of annoyed family

epics, nothing but episodic payback with
crescendoing spirals of blood blocking exactly

the same arteries and messing exactly
the same stony thoroughfares. This thinking

with things as they exist, what
good does it do anyone not

yet born? Back in my century,
back in the matter with me,

I flew, like other poets, we
signed our letters and sold them,

kept them, lost them, gave our
love to particular people, meant by

this something like I'm touching the
keys and this once they are

not as cold as some medieval
suet, blessed and eaten, damned and

waiting for the future where the
dead are already buried en masse

by judgments already made, beneath lobs
of fundamental meaning smashing bridges with

aimless accuracy, probing the most removed
non-readers for the smell of their

heirs. Give my love to their
particular cases in particular places, which

I can't see from here and
so have to lob the whole

mass into what looks illegible. Until
one day, a day that will

never die, since it only exists
in the past and the future,

with my body blocking the otherwise
perfect symmetry,

UNIVERSITY PRESS OF NEW ENGLAND publishes books under its own imprint and is the publisher for Brandeis University Press, Dartmouth College, Middlebury College Press, University of New Hampshire, Tufts University, and Wesleyan University Press.

ABOUT THE AUTHOR

Born in Youngstown, Ohio in 1947, Bob Perelman studied Classics at the University of Michigan, then, at the urging of Donald Hall, attended the Writers Workshop at the University of Iowa. In 1976 he and his wife, Francie Shaw, moved to San Francisco Bay Area, where they lived for fifteen years. With their two sons, they now live in Philadelphia where he teaches at the University of Pennsylvania.

In addition to his poetry, he has published critical works, including *The Marginalization of Poetry: Language Writing and Literary History* (Princeton University Press, 1996) and *The Trouble with Genius: Reading Pound, Joyce, Stein, and Zukofsky* (University of California Press, 1994). He has edited two collections of poets' talks: *Talks* (*Hills* 6/7) and *Writing/Talks* (Southern Illinois University Press, 1985).

LIBRARY OF CONGRESS CATALOGING-IN-PUBLICATION DATA
Perelman, Bob.
    Ten to one : selected poems / Bob Perelman.
        p.   cm. — (Wesleyan poetry)
    ISBN 0-8195-6387-0 (alk. paper). — ISBN 0-8195-6388-9 (pbk. :
alk. paper)
    I. Title. II. Series.
PS3566.E69125A6   1999
811'.54—dc21   99-34281